All About Pentagon: A Kid's Guide to America's Military Headquarters

Educational Books For Kids, Volume 49

Shah Rukh

Published by Shah Rukh, 2024.

While every precaution has been taken in the preparation of this book, the publisher assumes no responsibility for errors or omissions, or for damages resulting from the use of the information contained herein.

ALL ABOUT PENTAGON: A KID'S GUIDE TO AMERICA'S MILITARY HEADQUARTERS

First edition. November 15, 2024.

Copyright © 2024 Shah Rukh.

ISBN: 979-8230357353

Written by Shah Rukh.

Table of Contents

Prologue 1
Chapter 1: The Five-Sided Fortress 2
Chapter 2: Building a Pentagon Shaped Legend 5
Chapter 3: Inside the World's Largest Office Building 9
Chapter 4: The Pentagon's Secret Rooms 13
Chapter 5: Symbols of Strength and Strategy 17
Chapter 6: How the Pentagon Stays Secure 22
Chapter 7: The Brains Behind the Defense 27
Chapter 8: The People Who Work for the Pentagon 32
Chapter 9: From Planning to Protecting 38
Chapter 10: The Pentagon's Role in Wartime 44
Chapter 11: Technology and the Future of Defense 51
Chapter 12: Famous Moments at the Pentagon 57
Chapter 13: Solving Mysteries with Military Intelligence ... 62
Chapter 14: The Pentagon in Popular Culture 68
Chapter 15: Life Inside the Pentagon Walls 73
Chapter 16: How the Pentagon Supports the Armed Forces 79
Chapter 17: The Green Side of the Pentagon 85
Chapter 18: The History of the Pentagon's Construction ... 91
Chapter 19: How the Pentagon Keeps America Safe 95
Chapter 20: A Day in the Life of a Pentagon Worker 101
Epilogue 106

Prologue

Imagine a massive building shaped like a five-sided star, bustling with people, and filled with mysteries, high-tech gadgets, and important secrets. This place is known as the Pentagon, one of the most unique and powerful buildings in the world. But why does the Pentagon matter so much, and what really happens behind its five walls?

Built during World War II, the Pentagon has been at the center of some of the most important decisions and events in American history. It's the headquarters of the United States Department of Defense, where leaders and experts work day and night to protect and support the country. From creating strategies to protect our borders to planning missions around the world, the Pentagon is like the ultimate command center. But it's not all about action and technology; it's also a place where thousands of people work, learn, and develop ideas to keep the world a safer place.

In this book, you're going to take a journey inside the Pentagon. You'll learn how it was built, discover the secrets of its unique shape, meet the people who keep it running, and even explore the mysterious rooms and hidden passages that make it feel like something out of a spy movie. You'll find out how the Pentagon stays secure, what goes into planning a mission, and why it has become a symbol of strength and teamwork.

So, get ready to dive into the world of the Pentagon—where history, technology, and people come together to keep the United States safe and prepared. There's so much to learn and explore, and by the end of this book, you'll know just why the Pentagon is one of the most fascinating places in the world!

Chapter 1: The Five-Sided Fortress

Imagine a building so big and unique that it's shaped like a five-sided fortress, called the Pentagon! The Pentagon isn't just any building; it's the headquarters of the United States Department of Defense, where the nation's military plans, coordinates, and organizes to protect the country. When you look at the Pentagon from above, it's shaped like a giant five-pointed star or five-sided shape, which is why it's called "Pentagon," from the Greek word "pente," meaning five. This special shape isn't just for show. It was designed this way to help organize everything inside, with five equal sides, making it a fortress that's strong, compact, and efficient.

The Pentagon is in Arlington, Virginia, just across the Potomac River from Washington, D.C., so it's close to the U.S. capital. The building is enormous—one of the largest office buildings in the world, covering about 29 acres and taking up around 6.5 million square feet in total! That's like putting 115 football fields together! About 3.7 million of those square feet are used as offices, which is bigger than some entire towns! This space is necessary because more than 26,000 employees work at the Pentagon. These employees include military members, civilians, and contractors who are all dedicated to keeping the country safe and running its many important programs and projects.

What makes the Pentagon so unique is that it was designed with speed and efficiency in mind. Inside, the building has five rings, like layers of a cake, circling the middle. The five rings are labeled from A, which is the innermost ring, to E, which is the outermost ring. Each ring has corridors, stairways, and open spaces that let people move around quickly. In fact, someone could walk from one side of the Pentagon to the other in about seven minutes, even though the building is over 1,400 feet from side to side. There are also many entrances and exits, with 17.5 miles of hallways winding through it.

This allows people to move fast, whether they're going to a meeting, getting important documents, or sharing ideas with others.

The Pentagon is sometimes called a "fortress" because of its strong design and important role. Built in the early 1940s during World War II, it was constructed fast to keep up with the growing military needs of that time. It was completed in just 16 months, which was a record-breaking speed for such a massive structure. The designers used reinforced concrete, a type of building material mixed with steel, which makes it incredibly strong and sturdy. With this, the Pentagon was designed to stand the test of time and be ready for anything. It's like the heart of the country's defense, built to withstand all kinds of events.

Many people wonder why the Pentagon was designed to have five sides, and there's a fun story behind it. The original plan was for it to be built on land that was shaped like a pentagon, so it made sense to match the shape of the land. Even though the location changed later, they decided to keep the five-sided design because it was already planned out, and it turned out to be an ideal shape for the kind of work being done there. The five-sided shape not only allowed it to fit the massive number of people and departments it needed but also kept everything close together. So, the Pentagon was like a giant puzzle that had the perfect design to keep all the pieces connected.

Over the years, the Pentagon has become one of the most recognized buildings in the world, not only because of its size but also because of its significance. People who visit the Pentagon can take guided tours to learn more about its history and the role it plays. There's even a small museum inside with displays that teach visitors about military history and honor those who have served. This building stands as a reminder of the country's strength, resilience, and dedication to peace and safety. Inside its walls, important decisions are made every day that help keep the nation and its allies safe. It's no wonder that people call the Pentagon a fortress, as it's both a symbol and a center for America's defense system.

The Pentagon is not just a place of work; it's a symbol of protection. For many people in the United States, seeing the Pentagon reminds them of the dedication and teamwork of everyone who works there. Inside this five-sided fortress, people are constantly working on strategies to protect and defend, and they're always thinking about new ways to keep the country secure. It's a fortress in the truest sense, built to be strong, reliable, and ready for anything that comes its way.

Chapter 2: Building a Pentagon Shaped Legend

The Pentagon wasn't always a legendary building. In fact, the story of its creation is one full of determination, teamwork, and surprising twists. It all began in the early 1940s, right before the United States entered World War II. At that time, the U.S. military was growing quickly, and there was a huge need for a new headquarters that could fit all the departments and workers who were spread out across many different buildings. This scattered arrangement wasn't efficient, and the military needed a place where everyone could work together smoothly, share information, and make important decisions quickly. So, the idea of building one large headquarters was born, and they began planning something that would not only be big enough but would also become one of the most famous buildings in the world.

The original idea was to build the new headquarters on a plot of land by the Potomac River in Arlington, Virginia. That land was shaped like a five-sided pentagon, which inspired the building's design. Even though the building site changed to where the Pentagon stands today, the designers decided to keep the five-sided shape because it was so unique and practical. This design allowed them to fit many offices close together while keeping hallways short, so people wouldn't have to walk too far. This five-sided layout became an iconic design choice that would make the Pentagon recognizable around the world. The building itself was planned as something sturdy and impressive, built to last through time and different kinds of challenges.

Creating a building as large and complex as the Pentagon was a huge task, especially since the country needed it to be built quickly. To get this done, they hired more than 15,000 workers and put them on an intense schedule. The construction crews worked around the clock, with people working through the night to stay on track. It was one of the fastest construction projects of its kind. The whole building was completed in just 16 months, which was incredible given its size. The workers used a lot of concrete, mixing it with steel to make the building strong. In fact, the Pentagon used so much concrete that they were careful not to use up too much steel, as it was a valuable material needed for weapons and vehicles for the war. This careful use of resources made the Pentagon not only sturdy but also a smart, efficient building.

The building wasn't just about looking strong. Its design and layout had to be smart so that thousands of people could do their jobs quickly and easily. The Pentagon's five rings, labeled from A to E, each circle around the center, creating layers that make it easy for people to move from one section to another without getting lost. Even though the Pentagon has over 17 miles of hallways, someone can get from one side to the other in less than ten minutes because of this unique layout. The rings are connected by hallways called "spokes," which cut across the rings like the spokes of a wheel, giving people shortcuts to move faster. This design was intentional, allowing people to go from one meeting to another, share important information, and make decisions quickly.

The Pentagon officially opened on January 15, 1943, and people were in awe of its size and structure. At the time, it was the largest office building in the world, a record it held for a long time. The Pentagon could hold more than 26,000 people working under one roof, a number so large that it would be like having a whole town inside! Over the years, the building became more than just a place to work; it became a symbol of American strength and resilience. People around the country started to recognize the Pentagon not only for its size but also for what it stood for—a place where the United States would protect its freedom, plan its defenses, and think about ways to help other nations in times of need.

An interesting part of the Pentagon's legend is how it adapted over time. In the years after World War II, the Pentagon continued to serve as the center of the country's defense, but it also grew to include more technologies and updated facilities. As computers, phones, and other technologies advanced, so did the Pentagon, making sure it stayed a state-of-the-art building. In the 1990s, the Pentagon began a huge renovation to modernize the building, fixing up old parts and adding new, high-tech equipment. This modernization project took more than a decade, and they kept the building running the whole time, which was a big challenge. The goal was to keep the Pentagon as one of the most secure and efficient places for the country's defense.

The Pentagon also has a place in the hearts of many Americans because of the tragic events of September 11, 2001. On that day, the building was attacked, and a portion of it was heavily damaged. But almost immediately, workers began repairing and restoring it, symbolizing the country's strength and determination to overcome hardships. The restoration was completed in less than a year, and the Pentagon remained a powerful symbol of resilience. Since then, a beautiful memorial has been added outside the Pentagon, honoring the people who lost their lives on that day. This memorial is a reminder of the sacrifices made by many and the importance of the Pentagon in the country's story.

Today, the Pentagon stands as a living legend, representing the United States' commitment to peace, strength, and unity. People come from around the world to see this iconic building, and it remains one of the most well-known structures on the planet. Inside, the Pentagon is full of displays and information about the history of the U.S. military and the many people who have served the country. It's a place where history is made every day, as decisions that affect the country and even the world are discussed and planned. Even though it's made of concrete and steel, the Pentagon is also filled with stories of bravery, teamwork, and the determination to protect others. For all these reasons, the Pentagon has truly earned its status as a legendary building, a place that's strong in both design and purpose, standing as a fortress and a symbol of hope for people everywhere.

Chapter 3: Inside the World's Largest Office Building

Stepping inside the Pentagon, you're entering one of the world's most impressive office buildings, a place where thousands of people work each day to help keep the country safe. Imagine a small city inside a single building—that's what the Pentagon feels like! As the largest office building in the world, it has an incredible amount of space and is organized to make work efficient for everyone who is there. There are over 26,000 employees, including military members, civilians, and contractors, all working together under one massive roof. In fact, the Pentagon has over 6.5 million square feet of floor space, which is enough room to cover 115 football fields. Of that, about 3.7 million square feet are dedicated to offices alone. This makes it almost like a small country, with everyone working on important tasks to help run the U.S. Department of Defense.

The Pentagon's layout is one of the most unique aspects of the building. Inside, it's divided into five "rings," which are large, circular hallways layered inside one another. These rings are labeled A through E, starting from the innermost ring and moving outward. The rings are connected by passageways that work like spokes on a wheel, making it easy to move quickly from one ring to another. So, if you're going to a meeting on the other side of the building, you don't have to walk the entire way around; instead, you can use one of these passages to take a shortcut. Despite its enormous size, someone can walk from one side of the Pentagon to the other in less than ten minutes! This design, created with efficiency in mind, allows people to get where they need to be quickly, so they can focus on important tasks.

But the Pentagon isn't just hallways and offices. Inside, it has many surprising features that make it feel more like a small city than a typical workplace. For example, there's a large central courtyard right in the middle of the building. This outdoor space, which is about five acres in size, gives employees a place to relax, eat lunch, or get some fresh air. In fact, the courtyard is so big that some employees jokingly call it "Ground Zero," because they say it's like the heart of the building, where people can unwind. It's a reminder that even in a serious place like the Pentagon, taking breaks and enjoying nature is important.

Inside the Pentagon, there are also many facilities to make life easier for the people who work there. There are restaurants, snack bars, and even a food court with popular food chains so employees can grab a quick bite without leaving the building. There's also a small shopping center where people can buy essentials like office supplies, clothing, or gifts. There's even a post office, a bank, a barbershop, and a pharmacy—all the things you would find in a small town. These facilities make it easier for people working in the Pentagon to handle everyday errands and keep up with their work without having to go too far.

One of the most interesting parts of the Pentagon is its hallways, which are lined with displays, plaques, and historical exhibits. These displays tell the stories of important events in U.S. military history, honoring the bravery and sacrifice of those who have served. There are displays about the different branches of the military, like the Army, Navy, Air Force, and Marines, as well as exhibits about historic events, famous battles, and the accomplishments of military leaders. For those who work at the Pentagon, these displays are reminders of the important work they're part of and the history they help to protect and uphold. Visitors who come to the Pentagon can also see some of these exhibits, giving them a glimpse into the legacy and dedication that fills the building.

The Pentagon has a library that's one of the most extensive collections of military-related materials in the world. The Pentagon Library is a valuable resource, full of books, reports, and documents about military strategy, history, and world affairs. It's a place where researchers, historians, and military members can find information to help with planning and decision-making. This library makes the Pentagon not only a place of action and planning but also a place of learning, where people can dive deep into subjects that shape the way they think about security and defense.

The building also has a lot of technology to help people do their jobs. Each day, employees rely on computers, secure networks, and advanced communication tools to stay connected with people in other parts of the building and around the world. The Pentagon has its own secure communication systems to keep information private and protected. Since decisions made in the Pentagon affect not just the United States but also international relations, security is extremely important. To keep everything safe, there are many security checkpoints throughout the building, along with strict protocols to make sure that only authorized people have access to certain areas.

The Pentagon is home to the National Military Command Center, or NMCC, which is one of the most secure rooms in the entire building. This center acts as a hub for military operations, where leaders keep track of global events and stay prepared to respond to any situation at a moment's notice. Inside the NMCC, people monitor maps, data, and communication lines that allow them to see what's happening worldwide. If something urgent arises, this center can be used to connect top military leaders, allowing them to make quick decisions to keep the country safe. This room is like the nerve center of the Pentagon, connecting people to places around the world and ensuring that the Department of Defense is always ready.

Another important part of the Pentagon is its memorial areas. After the tragic events of September 11, 2001, when the Pentagon was attacked, a special memorial was created to honor those who lost their lives. This outdoor memorial has 184 benches, one for each person who passed away, and each bench is positioned to face either the Pentagon or the path of Flight 77, which struck the building. People visiting the

Pentagon can go to this peaceful spot to remember the lives lost and reflect on the impact of that day. The memorial reminds everyone of the bravery, unity, and resilience that the Pentagon stands for.

People who work at the Pentagon are dedicated to serving the country in many ways. While they may not all be soldiers on the front lines, their work supports military operations, plans strategies, and coordinates efforts to ensure that the United States remains safe. Inside the Pentagon, decisions are made that impact the entire nation and even the world. Whether it's through developing new technologies, helping communities affected by natural disasters, or planning for national defense, the people inside the Pentagon are working every day to make a difference.

In every corner of the Pentagon, there is a sense of purpose and responsibility. From the large central courtyard to the quiet, secure rooms like the NMCC, each area has a role in supporting the country's defense. The Pentagon is more than just a building; it's a hub of activity, planning, history, and dedication. The people inside this vast office building may be spread across five rings, countless corridors, and different departments, but they all share a common goal—to protect, serve, and uphold the values of the United States. Inside these walls, history is made, and every day brings new challenges, decisions, and achievements that shape the future.

Chapter 4: The Pentagon's Secret Rooms

The Pentagon is full of fascinating places, and some of the most interesting ones are the secret rooms and secure areas hidden deep within this massive building. These spaces aren't visible to just anyone, and only people with special clearance get to enter them. These rooms play a big role in keeping the country safe, and they're built to handle top-secret work. The Pentagon is home to some of the most critical command centers and intelligence rooms in the United States, designed to keep important information safe and secure. From the outside, you'd never know that such rooms exist, as they're cleverly hidden within the building's complex structure, often behind unmarked doors or deep within secured corridors.

One of the most famous secure rooms is the National Military Command Center, or NMCC. The NMCC is one of the Pentagon's most secure areas and serves as a central point for all military operations. It's a place where top military leaders can gather to monitor situations around the world. This center operates 24/7, meaning there are always people inside, keeping an eye on global events, military movements, and potential threats. Inside the NMCC, there are giant screens that show real-time maps, data, and live feeds from around the world. If something happens anywhere that could affect the United States, the NMCC is one of the first places to know. Military leaders use the NMCC to stay connected with other bases, submarines, ships, and aircraft in real-time, allowing them to make fast decisions when needed.

The NMCC isn't the only high-security room in the Pentagon. There are also rooms dedicated to intelligence gathering, where teams work to collect and analyze information about other countries, events, and possible risks. These intelligence rooms are filled with secure computers, special software, and high-tech equipment that lets analysts gather information from many sources. The people working in these rooms have access to classified information, which means they're trusted to handle details that most people can't see. By studying and understanding all this data, they can help the government make better decisions. The work done in these rooms is often very secret, but it's vital to national security.

Another secretive area in the Pentagon is the Secure Compartmented Information Facility, or SCIF, where super-sensitive information is discussed. SCIFs are specially designed to prevent anyone outside the room from listening in. They are often soundproof and have advanced security systems that block any devices that might try to intercept the conversation. Inside a SCIF, military and government officials discuss plans, share information, and make decisions about highly classified issues. Even cell phones and electronic devices are not allowed inside, as they could risk someone overhearing the discussions. SCIFs are used for meetings that involve serious topics, like international crises, intelligence reports, or planning military operations. For the people inside, the SCIFs are a place where they can speak freely, knowing that everything is kept secure.

Many people are also fascinated by the underground bunker, known as the "Pentagon basement," which is hidden beneath the main building. During the Cold War, when there was fear of nuclear threats, the Pentagon was designed to include safe rooms underground that could protect people if there was an attack. While a lot of these spaces remain unvisited and unknown by most employees, they are maintained and updated to ensure they're ready if needed. Some of these underground spaces hold important supplies and resources, so the Pentagon could keep working even during emergencies. Although not many details are publicly known, these underground rooms and tunnels help make the Pentagon one of the most secure buildings in the world.

Even though much of the Pentagon operates like any other office building, these secret rooms add a layer of mystery and purpose to the building. For example, there are secure vaults, some of which hold classified documents and historical records that aren't open to the public. These documents are carefully guarded and kept safe within the Pentagon's walls. Certain people, such as historians or intelligence officers, may occasionally access them if they have a reason. These vaults are designed to protect important records, which could include anything from plans and reports to valuable items connected to military history. The Pentagon even has secure areas where advanced technology is tested and studied, so new ideas can be developed to help the military prepare for future needs.

Another secretive feature of the Pentagon is its own command and control communications systems. These systems help people inside the Pentagon talk to military leaders around the world, using special, secure lines that are protected from outside interference. These lines are essential because they allow high-ranking officials to have private conversations about national security, without anyone else listening in. The communication rooms are set up with high-tech devices, protected networks, and secure encryption that ensures everything said remains private. This allows leaders to make quick decisions, share information, and respond to emergencies whenever they need to, day or night. Only specific people with the right security clearances are allowed to use these special communication rooms and equipment.

The Pentagon's emergency command centers are also highly secure areas, designed to handle any kind of crisis, whether it's a natural disaster, an attack, or another serious event. These command centers have backup power sources, secure connections, and advanced monitoring equipment that allows them to stay operational no matter what's happening outside. This means that even in the worst situations, the Pentagon can still function and communicate with others. These emergency centers are equipped with supplies and technology to make sure everything keeps running, which is important for keeping the country safe. Some of these rooms are hidden deeper within the building and can be accessed only by the people who need them, making them an important part of the Pentagon's defense structure.

There are also rooms where cybersecurity experts work, protecting the Pentagon from cyber-attacks. These rooms are guarded by technology experts who monitor the Pentagon's computer systems, looking for any signs of trouble. Since information in the Pentagon is valuable, it's a big target for hackers, and these experts work around the clock to keep everything safe. They use powerful computers, specialized software, and encrypted networks to protect data from being stolen. By constantly monitoring and defending the Pentagon's systems, they help prevent secrets from falling into the wrong hands. These cybersecurity rooms are some of the most high-tech places in the Pentagon and are vital for keeping the building's digital information secure.

Altogether, these secret rooms and secure spaces make the Pentagon a place full of mystery and security. While most people may never see these rooms or know exactly what happens inside, they are essential for protecting the country. The people who work in these spaces have special jobs that require a lot of responsibility and dedication, as they are trusted with some of the nation's most sensitive information. These secret rooms are like the hidden heart of the Pentagon, where critical decisions are made, strategies are planned, and security is always top priority. Each of these rooms adds to the Pentagon's status as a unique and powerful building, full of hidden spaces that help it remain the stronghold of the U.S. defense system.

Chapter 5: Symbols of Strength and Strategy

The Pentagon is much more than just a massive building; it's filled with symbols that represent strength, strategy, and the history of the United States military. Each corner, corridor, and even the shape of the building itself carries a story and a meaning that goes beyond what most people see. From the five-sided structure to the statues, plaques, and displays, the Pentagon is like a museum, fortress, and command center all rolled into one. It serves as a powerful reminder of the sacrifices made by countless men and women who have served their country, as well as the strategies that have protected the nation through times of peace and war.

One of the most striking symbols of strength in the Pentagon is its unique five-sided shape, which has become famous worldwide. When the Pentagon was first designed, the shape was chosen almost by accident, since the original plot of land was five-sided. But once they decided to keep this unique shape, it became an unforgettable symbol of the U.S. Department of Defense. The pentagon shape allows for more efficient movement and organization, with five rings of hallways that help connect the entire building. The five-sided structure has since become a symbol of balance, unity, and strategic thinking. Just as each side of the building connects seamlessly to form one unified structure, the different branches of the military work together within the Pentagon, cooperating and supporting each other's missions. This unity of design and purpose reflects how the U.S. military operates, combining strength and cooperation to protect the nation.

Walking through the Pentagon, you'll see flags representing each branch of the military—the Army, Navy, Air Force, Marines, and Coast Guard—each of which has its own symbol, history, and traditions. These flags are displayed proudly in many places within the building as a reminder of the unique strengths and responsibilities each branch brings to the nation's defense. The flags also symbolize the honor and loyalty of those who serve. Each color and emblem on these flags has a special meaning, whether it's the navy blue of the Air Force representing the sky or the crossed anchors on the Coast Guard flag symbolizing their maritime duty. Seeing these flags displayed side by side reminds people that even though each branch is different, they all work together toward the same goal.

Throughout the Pentagon, there are many plaques and memorials dedicated to the brave individuals who have served in the military, especially those who gave their lives in service to the country. These plaques, which are placed in hallways and near important offices, are symbols of honor and sacrifice. Some are dedicated to specific units, battles, or individuals who have made a lasting impact. For example, the "Hall of Heroes" is a special area within the Pentagon that honors all recipients of the Medal of Honor, the highest award given to members of the U.S. military for acts of bravery and courage. The names and stories of these heroes are displayed on the walls, serving as inspiration to everyone who walks by and reminding them of the courage it takes to defend the nation.

There are also large, detailed displays in the Pentagon that tell the story of the United States military's history, from the earliest days of the Revolutionary War to modern-day missions around the world. These displays include models, artifacts, maps, and historical photographs that highlight important battles, key leaders, and the development of military technology over time. Some of these exhibits show uniforms and equipment used in the past, while others display modern tools and vehicles. These displays are symbols of strategy, showing how the military has adapted and grown over centuries to meet new challenges and protect the country. Visitors who see these exhibits gain a sense of the long, proud history of the U.S. military and its strategic importance throughout the world.

One of the most significant symbols of strength within the Pentagon is the September 11th Memorial, located outside the building. This memorial was built to honor the lives lost when the Pentagon was attacked on September 11, 2001. The memorial consists of 184 benches, each representing one of the victims of the attack, arranged in a peaceful outdoor setting near the site where the plane struck. Each bench has the name of one of the victims engraved on it, and they are positioned in a way that represents their age, from the youngest, who was only three years old, to the oldest. This memorial is a solemn symbol of resilience and remembrance, reminding people of the sacrifices made on that tragic day and the strength the Pentagon showed in rebuilding and continuing its mission. It's a place where visitors can pause, reflect, and honor the bravery of those who were lost, as well as the determination of those who worked to restore the Pentagon after the attack.

Inside the Pentagon, the National Military Command Center, or NMCC, serves as another symbol of strategy and readiness. This command center is where important decisions are made, and it operates around the clock, every single day of the year. It's a secure area filled with advanced technology, maps, and communication equipment that allows military leaders to monitor global events and respond to any emergency. The NMCC stands as a symbol of preparedness, showing the country's commitment to staying vigilant and ready to defend against any threat. For those who work in the Pentagon, the NMCC is a powerful reminder of their responsibility to be always prepared and proactive in protecting the country.

There are also beautiful works of art and statues throughout the Pentagon that capture the spirit of service and strength. Some of these works are tributes to famous leaders, such as General George Washington or Admiral Chester Nimitz, who played crucial roles in shaping the U.S. military. Other statues and sculptures represent broader concepts like liberty, honor, and sacrifice. These pieces of art, along with murals and paintings, add a sense of pride and dignity to the building. Each artwork tells a story, from portraits of soldiers in action to scenes depicting important moments in military history. They serve as symbols of the bravery and dedication of everyone who serves in the military, helping to remind people of the values the Pentagon stands for.

The building's massive, solid construction is itself a symbol of strength. Made of concrete and steel, the Pentagon was built to last, and its design is meant to be strong enough to withstand various challenges. When it was constructed during World War II, engineers chose materials that would make it durable and stable, so the building would stand the test of time. After the 9/11 attack, the Pentagon was repaired and strengthened further, showing the resilience of the building and the people who work within it. Today, the Pentagon's strong foundation and durable structure serve as a symbol of the military's dedication to standing strong, no matter what challenges may come.

Finally, the Pentagon represents a place where strategy and strength come together. Every day, military leaders, analysts, and specialists gather here to discuss, plan, and coordinate efforts that impact not just the United States but also allies and regions around the world. The Pentagon serves as a center for strategic thinking, where people study maps, assess situations, and develop plans that protect lives and support allies. It's a place of decision-making, where strategies are created to respond to conflicts, protect resources, and defend freedoms. For many, the Pentagon is not only a physical building but a symbol of the powerful ideas and strategic thinking that help keep the nation safe and secure.

As the Pentagon continues to grow and adapt, it remains a lasting symbol of the United States' commitment to protecting its people, honoring its history, and planning for the future. Whether through its architecture, its memorials, or its command centers, the Pentagon stands as a fortress of strength and a beacon of strategy, dedicated to preserving the country's values and upholding peace. Each person working there contributes to a legacy of courage, intelligence, and determination, ensuring that the Pentagon remains a powerful symbol of the United States for generations to come.

Chapter 6: How the Pentagon Stays Secure

The Pentagon is one of the most secure buildings in the world, and it has to be, since it's where the United States Department of Defense plans and coordinates much of the country's defense. With over 20,000 people working inside, many of whom handle sensitive or classified information, the Pentagon needs to have multiple layers of security to keep everyone safe and prevent unauthorized people from accessing important areas. There's no single trick or magic system that makes the Pentagon so secure—it's actually a combination of many different types of protections, each designed to address specific threats. From high-tech alarms to specially trained guards, the Pentagon has put in place a security system that is constantly updated and improved to stay ahead of any potential threats.

One of the most basic parts of the Pentagon's security is the perimeter around the building. When you look at the Pentagon from above, you'll see that it's surrounded by a large area of open land, which gives security teams plenty of space to monitor and watch for any suspicious activity. This space, called a "buffer zone," helps keep the Pentagon safe from anyone who might try to approach too closely. There are also security fences, barriers, and guard stations surrounding this buffer zone. Visitors to the Pentagon must go through multiple checkpoints before they even reach the building, which helps ensure that only people with permission can get close. This outer ring of security is staffed by guards and security cameras 24/7, so the building is always under watch.

To enter the Pentagon itself, every visitor needs to pass through a carefully controlled entrance. Security at these entrances is extremely tight. Visitors need to show identification, and in some cases, they must have their fingerprints or other biometric information checked.

Military and civilian staff also go through checks each day, even if they work there regularly. Metal detectors and X-ray machines are used to screen bags and personal items to make sure no dangerous objects get inside. Every person who enters is recorded in the system, so the Pentagon keeps track of everyone who is on the premises at all times. This helps security teams know exactly who's inside and where they are, just in case any issues arise.

Once inside, security measures don't stop. The Pentagon uses advanced surveillance technology, including thousands of security cameras placed strategically throughout the building, in hallways, meeting rooms, and even the parking areas. These cameras allow security staff to monitor nearly every part of the building, ensuring that no unusual activity goes unnoticed. The Pentagon also uses motion sensors, which can detect when someone is in a certain area and alert security if they're somewhere they shouldn't be. This way, if someone tries to access a restricted area, security will be notified immediately. These sensors are part of a high-tech alarm system that keeps watch over every floor, every room, and every corridor.

Some areas of the Pentagon are more secure than others, especially rooms where classified information is discussed or stored. These secure rooms are often protected by additional locks, keycard access, and biometric scans like fingerprint or retina scans. Only people with the right level of security clearance are allowed to enter these spaces, and sometimes even specific clearance isn't enough—some rooms require special permission for each visit. Secure rooms, often called SCIFs (Sensitive Compartmented Information Facilities), are also built to be soundproof, so conversations inside cannot be overheard by anyone outside the room. This is particularly important for meetings where top-secret information is discussed.

Technology plays a big role in keeping the Pentagon secure. The building has its own internal network for communication and data sharing, and this network is heavily protected against cyber threats.

Cybersecurity experts work around the clock to monitor and defend against hackers who might try to access sensitive information. They use special software to detect any suspicious activity on the network and take action if they spot any risks. The Pentagon's cybersecurity team is constantly testing and improving its defenses, as cyber threats change and grow more advanced over time. This part of the Pentagon's security is especially important, since it protects data and plans that could affect national security.

In addition to technology, human guards play a crucial role in the Pentagon's security. The Pentagon Force Protection Agency, or PFPA, is responsible for keeping the building and its people safe. The PFPA officers are highly trained and have special knowledge about how to respond to any kind of security issue that could come up, whether it's a natural disaster, an attack, or an emergency inside the building. They patrol the building day and night, watching for anything unusual and responding quickly to any alarms. These officers know the Pentagon inside and out, and they're prepared for a wide range of scenarios, from fires to intruders. Some of them are even trained in bomb detection and work with specially trained dogs that can sniff out explosives.

The Pentagon also has detailed emergency plans to handle unexpected events. For instance, if there's a fire or a natural disaster, there are evacuation plans in place to help people get out quickly and safely. There are also special rooms, known as safe rooms, located throughout the building. These rooms are designed to protect people in case of an emergency, providing a safe place for people to gather if they can't evacuate right away. The Pentagon runs regular drills and training exercises for its staff so that everyone knows what to do in an emergency. This helps ensure that, even if something unexpected happens, the people inside the Pentagon are prepared to handle it calmly and efficiently.

In recent years, the Pentagon has added even more advanced security features. For example, facial recognition technology is now being used to identify people entering the building, making it even harder for unauthorized visitors to get inside. This technology can quickly scan and match a person's face with their identity, providing another layer of protection beyond traditional ID cards or badges. This is particularly helpful in ensuring that people are who they say they are, adding another layer of verification before allowing entry.

Outside the Pentagon, there are also precautions in place to protect against drone threats. Drones, or small unmanned flying devices, could be used to spy or even attempt attacks, so the Pentagon has implemented special technology to detect and disable drones if they get too close. This system can track a drone's flight path, identify its type, and even take control of it if necessary, making sure it doesn't pose a risk to the building or its people. With the rise in drone usage worldwide, these types of protections are essential for a high-profile building like the Pentagon.

Even the design of the building itself helps keep it secure. The Pentagon was built with thick concrete walls, making it extremely durable and difficult to damage. After the 9/11 attack, additional reinforcements were added to improve its structural integrity, so today, the Pentagon is even stronger than it was before. These reinforced walls are resistant to many types of attacks, making it difficult for anyone to harm the building with conventional means. The layout of the building also contributes to security, as it's designed in a way that helps contain and control access to various areas, making it harder for anyone to move around without authorization.

Finally, the Pentagon relies on a constant process of review and improvement to maintain its security. Security experts regularly assess the building's defenses and look for ways to make them even better. They study the latest threats, test new technology, and work closely with other government agencies to ensure that the Pentagon remains as secure as possible. By staying up-to-date with the latest security measures and adapting to new challenges, the Pentagon can continue to protect both the people who work there and the vital information it holds.

All these measures come together to create a security system that is incredibly thorough and reliable. From the guards at the gates to the cybersecurity experts monitoring digital threats, every layer of protection plays an important part. The Pentagon's security isn't just about keeping people out—it's about creating a safe space where the nation's defense leaders can work confidently, knowing they are protected. The combination of physical, digital, and strategic security measures helps make the Pentagon one of the safest places in the world, and a symbol of strength and protection for the United States.

Chapter 7: The Brains Behind the Defense

The Pentagon is often called the "brains" of the United States defense, because it's where some of the most important decisions about national security are made. Inside this massive five-sided building, thousands of people work together to plan, strategize, and ensure the country's safety. The people working here come from different branches of the military—the Army, Navy, Air Force, Marines, and Coast Guard—as well as civilian departments. They handle everything from researching new technology to planning missions and protecting against cyberattacks. The Pentagon is not just a building; it's a command center where some of the brightest minds in defense gather to solve complex problems, often under intense pressure. These individuals dedicate themselves to keeping the country safe from both known threats and new challenges that arise around the world.

The Pentagon is home to the Department of Defense, or DoD, which is the main agency responsible for the military and defense of the United States. The Secretary of Defense, one of the President's closest advisors, leads the DoD from the Pentagon. The Secretary of Defense is in charge of making big decisions that affect the entire military and is also responsible for advising the President on issues related to national security. This position requires deep knowledge of military strategies, politics, and global affairs, as well as the ability to make tough decisions quickly and accurately. The Secretary of Defense works alongside top military leaders, known as the Joint Chiefs of Staff, who represent each branch of the military. Together, they form a kind of "brain trust" for the country's defense, drawing on their experiences, skills, and insights to help guide the military.

The Joint Chiefs of Staff are a group of high-ranking officers who play a crucial role in the Pentagon's decision-making. Each branch of the military has a chief, such as the Chief of Staff of the Army or the Chief of Naval Operations, and these chiefs come together to provide advice on military matters. The Chairman of the Joint Chiefs of Staff, who is the highest-ranking military officer in the country, leads this group. This team is responsible for advising the President, the Secretary of Defense, and other key leaders on how best to use the military to protect the country. They consider everything from troop movements and battle strategies to the latest intelligence on possible threats. While the Joint Chiefs do not have direct control over military operations, their recommendations are highly influential and help shape the decisions that affect how the U.S. military operates around the world.

Inside the Pentagon, experts work in different offices and departments focused on various aspects of defense. For instance, there are intelligence analysts who study information from around the world, looking for signs of potential dangers. These analysts gather data from satellites, reports, and sometimes even spies, piecing together clues that help predict what might happen next. They monitor situations in other countries, paying close attention to regions where conflicts are brewing or where there's political instability that could affect the U.S. Intelligence analysts work closely with military planners to create strategies for responding to these situations, whether it means sending troops to a certain area, preparing for potential attacks, or strengthening alliances with other countries. Their work often goes unnoticed by the public, but it is essential for making sure the military is ready for any situation.

Another key part of the Pentagon's "brains" is the team responsible for research and development. This group focuses on creating and improving technology that will give the military an edge. From advanced weapons systems to protective equipment, military technology has to be both powerful and reliable. Engineers, scientists, and technologists at the Pentagon work on projects like drones, cybersecurity, and artificial intelligence. They collaborate with private companies, universities, and research institutions to stay on the cutting edge of technology. Many of the tools they develop, like GPS or the internet, actually start as military projects before eventually becoming available to the public. The research and development teams at the Pentagon are always looking for ways to improve the military's capabilities, so the country is prepared for both current and future challenges.

Cybersecurity is another major focus area for the Pentagon. In today's world, protecting the country doesn't just mean defending physical borders; it also involves safeguarding against cyber threats. The Pentagon has a dedicated team of cybersecurity experts who monitor networks and systems for signs of hacking attempts or other digital attacks. These experts are part of the U.S. Cyber Command, a branch of the military that specializes in defending against cyber threats. They work around the clock, using advanced software to detect suspicious activity and prevent hackers from accessing sensitive information. This job is incredibly important because cyber threats can come from anywhere in the world, and a successful attack could disrupt important systems or compromise national security. The cybersecurity team's work is one of the newer but essential "brains" of the Pentagon's defense strategy.

In addition to military and technology experts, the Pentagon employs many civilians who bring specialized knowledge in areas like finance, logistics, and health care. For instance, managing the military budget is a huge responsibility, since it involves billions of dollars that must be spent wisely to maintain the readiness of the armed forces. Financial experts at the Pentagon work on everything from buying new equipment to paying service members. They make sure that every dollar is used effectively to support the military's mission. Similarly, logistics experts focus on getting supplies—like food, fuel, and medical equipment—to troops stationed around the world. Without these essential supplies, military operations could come to a standstill, so logistics experts ensure that everything needed for a mission is in place and arrives on time. These civilian experts are the backbone of the Pentagon's operations, ensuring that all parts of the military have what they need to function smoothly.

The Pentagon is also home to diplomats and foreign policy experts who help maintain good relationships with allies. These experts work closely with other countries to build partnerships, exchange information, and sometimes plan joint military exercises. Having strong relationships with other nations helps the U.S. military operate more effectively and provides additional support during times of crisis. For example, NATO, or the North Atlantic Treaty Organization, is an alliance of countries that agree to defend each other if one of them is attacked. The Pentagon's foreign policy team works on keeping these alliances strong, so the United States has friends and allies who will stand by it in times of need.

Planning and preparation are a big part of the Pentagon's day-to-day activities. Military planners analyze possible scenarios, from natural disasters to full-scale conflicts, and create plans for how to respond to each situation. These plans can take months or even years to develop, and they must be flexible enough to adapt as situations change. Planners consider everything from how many troops will be needed to what kind of equipment they should bring. They also look at factors like terrain, weather, and the possible actions of an enemy. By carefully thinking through these details, military planners help ensure that when the time comes for action, the military can move quickly and efficiently. This planning process is a vital part of the Pentagon's brainpower, allowing the U.S. to be ready for a wide range of situations.

At the heart of the Pentagon's mission is the commitment to keep the nation safe. The people who work there take their responsibilities seriously because they know that their decisions can affect millions of lives. Every day, they face complex challenges and make difficult choices, knowing that their actions are critical to the security of the country. The Pentagon's "brains" work in sync, combining knowledge, skill, and determination to create a defense strategy that is strong and effective. From top generals and civilian experts to young analysts just starting their careers, everyone at the Pentagon plays a role in this mission. It takes teamwork and dedication to coordinate such a massive operation, and the people who work in the Pentagon are committed to doing whatever it takes to protect the nation.

The Pentagon's role as the "brains" behind the defense doesn't just happen during times of conflict. Even in peacetime, the Pentagon is constantly studying, planning, and preparing. By staying vigilant and adaptable, they ensure that the military is always ready for whatever challenges the future may hold. The Pentagon is a unique place, full of knowledge, innovation, and commitment, where people come together to make the tough choices that keep the country safe.

Chapter 8: The People Who Work for the Pentagon

The Pentagon is like a huge city of its own, with thousands of people working together to support the United States military and make sure that the country stays safe. It's easy to think that only military personnel work in the Pentagon, but the truth is that people from many different professions and backgrounds come together there. Some wear military uniforms, representing the Army, Navy, Air Force, Marines, and Coast Guard, while others wear civilian clothing because they're not part of the armed forces. All of these people work as a team, each person bringing unique skills to the Pentagon's mission. Whether they are planning military operations, analyzing intelligence, managing budgets, or designing technology, they all play important roles in making sure everything runs smoothly and efficiently.

The Pentagon is home to many high-ranking military officers who are in charge of making major decisions. Some of these leaders have spent decades in the military, and they use their experience to guide strategies and make tough calls. Among these leaders are the Joint Chiefs of Staff, a group of the top military officers from each branch of the armed forces. These officers work closely with the Secretary of Defense, who is the highest civilian official in charge of the Department of Defense. Together, they advise the President and make decisions that affect the entire U.S. military. This leadership team doesn't just focus on day-to-day decisions; they also think about long-term goals and challenges, making plans that will shape the future of the military for years to come. Their jobs require deep knowledge of global issues, military tactics, and government policies.

Besides the leaders at the top, there are countless other military personnel working at the Pentagon who handle all kinds of responsibilities. Some are planners who develop strategies for different missions. They study possible situations and come up with step-by-step plans that explain how the military should respond if certain events happen. These plans take a lot of research and careful thinking, and they have to be very detailed. The planners need to think about what kinds of troops and equipment will be needed, how supplies will be delivered, and how the mission will fit with other goals. Planning isn't just about predicting the future; it's also about making sure that everyone is prepared for anything.

In addition to planners, the Pentagon also has intelligence analysts. These analysts play a critical role because they gather information about potential threats from around the world. Intelligence analysts use data from satellites, reports, and sometimes even spies to understand what's happening in other countries. They try to figure out if any groups or governments might pose a threat to the U.S. by studying patterns, looking for clues, and piecing together bits of information. If they spot something that could be a threat, they share it with military leaders so that the U.S. can prepare or take action. Intelligence analysts have to be very careful and precise because even a small mistake could lead to a misunderstanding or a missed opportunity to prevent a problem.

There are also many people at the Pentagon who work in communications, making sure that information is shared clearly and quickly. Communication experts help keep everyone on the same page by coordinating messages between different branches of the military, other government agencies, and sometimes even other countries. They also help manage public information, so they are responsible for explaining the military's actions and decisions to the American public. Communication experts play a huge role in building trust and keeping people informed, which is especially important during times of crisis or conflict. They create reports, handle media inquiries, and help make sure that the right information reaches the right people at the right time.

The Pentagon wouldn't be able to run without logistics experts. These people are in charge of getting supplies, equipment, and people where they need to be, both within the Pentagon and all around the world. They coordinate shipments of food, fuel, medicine, and other essentials to ensure that troops in the field have what they need. For instance, if there's a mission happening in a remote part of the world, the logistics team figures out how to get all the necessary supplies to that location. This might involve ships, airplanes, or trucks, and each mode of transport requires its own careful planning. Logistics experts often have to solve complicated problems quickly, like figuring out alternative routes if weather or other obstacles get in the way. Their work is crucial to keeping the military running smoothly, and they are often considered the backbone of military operations.

The Pentagon is also filled with people who work in research and development, constantly coming up with new technologies to improve the military's capabilities. Scientists, engineers, and technologists work on a wide range of projects, from creating more advanced communication systems to developing protective gear that can withstand extreme conditions. Some of them work on futuristic projects like artificial intelligence and robotics, hoping to give the U.S. military an edge in future conflicts. Research and development experts test new equipment, study potential weaknesses, and make sure everything is as safe and effective as possible. Many of the technologies they develop eventually become useful outside the military as well. For example, GPS technology, which most people use today for navigation, was initially developed for the military.

Another essential group of people in the Pentagon is the cybersecurity team. These experts protect the Pentagon's networks from cyberattacks, which is especially important in today's world where digital threats are becoming more common. Cybersecurity experts work tirelessly to stop hackers from accessing sensitive information or disrupting important systems. They use special software to monitor network activity, detect unusual patterns, and prevent unauthorized access. Cybersecurity is a rapidly evolving field, and these experts constantly update their skills to stay ahead of new types of threats. The work they do is vital to national security, as a single successful cyberattack could potentially cause a lot of harm.

There are also many civilian employees who work at the Pentagon, helping with tasks like managing finances, organizing medical care, and maintaining facilities. Financial experts at the Pentagon oversee a massive budget that includes everything from salaries for soldiers to purchases of high-tech equipment. They make sure that funds are spent wisely and that every dollar is used to support the military's mission. Health care workers provide medical services and develop health policies to keep military personnel and their families healthy. Maintenance workers keep the Pentagon building itself in good condition, handling everything from repairs to daily cleaning. These jobs may not sound as exciting as planning missions or gathering intelligence, but they are absolutely essential. Without these behind-the-scenes workers, the Pentagon wouldn't be able to function as smoothly as it does.

Another group of people who are important to the Pentagon's mission are diplomats and foreign relations experts. These individuals work to maintain good relationships with allies and manage interactions with other countries. They work closely with the military to plan joint exercises, share information, and build partnerships. Diplomatic experts often speak multiple languages and have deep knowledge of the cultures and politics of other countries, which helps them communicate and negotiate effectively. When the Pentagon needs to coordinate with an ally or find a peaceful solution to a conflict, these diplomats play a crucial role. They help build trust with other nations, which can make it easier to prevent conflicts or work together in times of need.

Many of the people working at the Pentagon are highly trained specialists, but there are also people there who are just starting their careers. The Pentagon is a place where new employees can learn a lot and gain valuable experience. Some young officers and recent college graduates join the Pentagon to learn about defense strategy, international relations, or advanced technology. They may start out assisting with research, helping to organize meetings, or preparing reports. As they gain experience, they take on more responsibilities and eventually become experts in their fields. The Pentagon values new perspectives, and younger employees often bring fresh ideas that can lead to new solutions.

Everyone at the Pentagon, no matter their role, shares a common goal: to support the country's defense and ensure that the military is prepared for any challenge. They often work long hours, tackling difficult problems that require careful planning, teamwork, and quick thinking. Their work can be demanding, but it's also incredibly meaningful. They know that what they do each day has a direct impact on the security of the United States. Working at the Pentagon requires dedication, patience, and a sense of responsibility. Many of the people there feel proud to serve their country, whether they're in uniform or working as civilians.

At the end of the day, the Pentagon is more than just a building—it's a community of people who bring their skills and knowledge together for a common purpose. It's a place where leaders, analysts, planners, scientists, engineers, and many others work side by side to tackle some of the toughest challenges in national defense. Each person, no matter their specific role, contributes to the larger mission of keeping the country safe. The work they do is complex, but it's all aimed at a single goal: to protect the people of the United States. Whether they're handling logistics, developing new technology, managing budgets, or gathering intelligence, the people of the

Pentagon are committed to supporting the military and ensuring the security of the nation.

Chapter 9: From Planning to Protecting

When it comes to defending the United States, the Pentagon is where it all begins. From planning military missions to protecting national interests, the Pentagon is at the center of almost everything related to America's defense. The Pentagon's work includes a wide range of activities, from figuring out how to respond to different threats to developing new technologies and training soldiers. Every day, experts from all sorts of fields come together to plan and prepare for situations they hope will never happen, but that they are ready for just in case. This work is crucial because a well-prepared military can help prevent conflicts from happening in the first place, and if they do happen, it's vital to respond as quickly and effectively as possible.

Planning is one of the first steps in the Pentagon's process of protecting the country. Military planners think about every possible scenario that might require a response, whether it's a natural disaster, a conflict with another country, or a sudden crisis that could affect American lives. These planners have to imagine every detail, from where troops will go, to how they'll get there, to what supplies they'll need once they arrive. They work through potential challenges, like rough terrain or extreme weather, and come up with solutions to make sure the mission can succeed no matter what. It's almost like putting together a giant puzzle, but one where the pieces are constantly changing, and there's always something new to consider.

To prepare for all kinds of situations, planners study intelligence reports that provide information about what's happening in different parts of the world. Intelligence analysts gather data from many sources, including satellites, ground reports, and sometimes even information shared by allies. They look for patterns that might indicate a potential threat, such as unusual troop movements or signs of political instability in a certain country. If they notice something concerning, they alert the planners so they can begin considering possible responses. This information is critical because it helps the military be proactive—taking steps before a threat becomes a serious problem. The earlier they can prepare, the more options they have, which can sometimes even mean finding a way to resolve issues peacefully.

Once the intelligence has been gathered, military planners start mapping out possible responses. For example, if there's a threat of conflict in a certain region, they might create a plan to move troops and equipment there as a deterrent. They consider factors like the number of troops required, the best type of equipment, and how long the mission might last. Planners also think about how to keep service members safe during the mission, including what kind of medical support might be needed and how to handle emergencies. These plans are like roadmaps, showing every step needed to complete a mission successfully. They include backup options too, because things don't always go as expected. Having multiple options allows the military to adjust if something unexpected happens.

Technology is a big part of the Pentagon's planning and protection efforts. Engineers and scientists work on developing new tools that can give the military an advantage in various situations. For instance, they might design drones that can gather information without putting people in harm's way, or they might create protective gear that can withstand extreme conditions. Research teams at the Pentagon are always trying to stay one step ahead by experimenting with new ideas, testing prototypes, and improving existing technology. These technological advancements often give the military a significant advantage in missions, making it easier to gather information, communicate securely, and keep service members safe. Much of this technology also eventually benefits the public, as innovations like GPS and the internet, which started as military projects, became widely used around the world.

Training is another essential part of the Pentagon's approach to planning and protecting. The Pentagon ensures that all service members are well-prepared for whatever challenges they might face. Military personnel go through rigorous training that includes everything from basic skills to advanced tactics. They practice how to work together as a team, how to use their equipment, and how to respond in high-pressure situations. They also participate in exercises that simulate real-world scenarios, allowing them to put their training into practice in controlled settings. Some of these exercises are incredibly realistic, involving helicopters, tanks, and sometimes even live ammunition, so that soldiers know exactly what to expect in a real mission. The goal is to make sure everyone is confident and capable, no matter what they encounter in the field.

In addition to training American forces, the Pentagon also collaborates with other countries to strengthen global security. The Pentagon often works with allies to conduct joint training exercises and share strategies, which helps build trust and improve cooperation. For example, NATO, the North Atlantic Treaty Organization, is a military alliance that includes the United States and many European countries. When NATO members train together, they learn how to coordinate their efforts so they can act as a unified force if needed. This type of international cooperation makes it easier for the U.S. and its allies to work together in times of crisis, whether it's a natural disaster or a security threat.

The Pentagon is also heavily involved in cybersecurity, which is an increasingly important part of national defense. Cybersecurity experts at the Pentagon work to protect the nation's computer systems and networks from cyberattacks. They constantly monitor for unusual activity that might indicate someone is trying to hack into sensitive information. These experts use complex software and encryption tools to secure data, and they respond quickly to any signs of an attack. Cybersecurity is a unique kind of defense because threats can come from anywhere in the world, and they often happen silently, without any warning. The cybersecurity team is essential to the Pentagon's mission because so much of modern warfare involves digital technology. Protecting computer systems is just as important as defending physical locations, especially as technology continues to play a bigger role in both military operations and everyday life.

Part of the Pentagon's job is also to keep a close eye on the development of new threats. As technology changes, new kinds of weapons and tactics become possible, and the Pentagon must stay up-to-date to protect against them. For example, as countries around the world develop more advanced drones and artificial intelligence, the Pentagon is studying these technologies to understand how they might be used in both offensive and defensive situations. Sometimes this means developing new defenses, like anti-drone technology, to counter potential threats. This kind of forward-thinking approach is vital to keeping the military prepared for whatever challenges the future may bring.

Another important part of the Pentagon's work is preparing for natural disasters and other emergencies. The military often assists in disaster relief efforts, both in the United States and around the world. Planners create detailed strategies for how to respond if a hurricane, earthquake, or other disaster strikes. They figure out what kind of supplies will be needed, such as food, water, and medical equipment, and how to transport these supplies to affected areas. Sometimes, the military sets up temporary hospitals or shelters to help people in need. By planning for these situations in advance, the Pentagon can respond quickly and effectively, helping to save lives and provide relief to communities in crisis.

Planning for protection isn't just about reacting to threats—it's also about preventing them. The Pentagon works on strategies to keep potential conflicts from turning into bigger problems. Diplomats and foreign relations experts at the Pentagon work with other countries to build strong relationships and find peaceful solutions to disagreements. By talking and negotiating with other countries, they try to prevent conflicts before they even begin. When successful, this kind of diplomacy can help create a more stable and peaceful world. These efforts are important because every time the Pentagon can prevent a conflict, it reduces the need to send soldiers into harm's way and allows countries to focus on growth and cooperation instead.

The Pentagon's efforts to protect the country also extend to the home front. Military police and security personnel work to safeguard Pentagon facilities, military bases, and important infrastructure across the country. They ensure that only authorized personnel have access to sensitive areas, and they monitor for any suspicious activities that might pose a risk to national security. In addition to physical security, the Pentagon has teams that prepare for biological and chemical threats, including potential attacks on U.S. soil. These teams are trained to respond to incidents involving hazardous materials, making sure that they can protect people and neutralize dangers effectively. Their work is crucial in maintaining safety both within the Pentagon and for the public.

The Pentagon's commitment to protecting the country doesn't stop after a plan is made or a mission is complete. Teams at the Pentagon evaluate past missions and exercises to learn from them and improve future operations. They look at what went well, what could have been done differently, and how new strategies might make the military even more effective. This process of constant learning and improvement helps the Pentagon stay prepared, making sure the military is ready for whatever comes next. By learning from the past and planning for the future, the Pentagon ensures that the U.S. defense remains strong and adaptable.

Every part of the Pentagon's planning and protecting efforts relies on teamwork. It takes many different types of experts—military officers, analysts, engineers, scientists, and many others—all working together to create a complete defense strategy. Each person brings a different skill set, and they rely on one another to get the job done.

The process involves careful coordination, clear communication, and a shared commitment to protecting the country. The people at the Pentagon understand that their work is bigger than any one individual; it's a joint effort that depends on everyone doing their part.

The Pentagon's mission to protect the United States is complex and constantly evolving. From planning detailed military strategies to responding to natural disasters and preventing cyberattacks, the Pentagon's work covers a vast range of responsibilities. Each decision made within those five walls has the potential to impact the entire country, and sometimes even the world. The people working at the Pentagon take this responsibility seriously, dedicating their time and expertise to making sure that the military is always ready, always prepared, and always one step ahead of any threat. Through planning, preparation, and teamwork, the Pentagon plays an essential role in keeping the country safe and secure.

Chapter 10: The Pentagon's Role in Wartime

When the United States is involved in a war or military conflict, the Pentagon becomes the central hub where everything related to planning, operations, and support is managed. It's not just a building; it's like the brain of the entire U.S. military, making sure that each part of the armed forces—whether it's the Army, Navy, Air Force, Marines, or Coast Guard—can work together smoothly. The Pentagon's role in wartime is both intense and incredibly important because the decisions made within its five walls can have major impacts on the battlefield, on soldiers, and on the country as a whole. Every step, from deciding on strategies to coordinating troop movements, is carefully considered and planned by experts at the Pentagon, all working together to ensure success and safety.

At the heart of the Pentagon's role during wartime are its top leaders, including high-ranking military officers and government officials. Some of the most critical figures are the Joint Chiefs of Staff, who are the top military leaders from each branch of the armed forces. They work alongside the Secretary of Defense, the highest-ranking civilian leader in charge of military matters. Together, they analyze the situation, discuss the options, and advise the President on the best course of action. Their job is to take in a vast amount of information, including intelligence reports and updates from the battlefield, and turn it into a clear, actionable plan. The President has the ultimate authority to make major decisions about going to war or conducting specific operations, but he relies heavily on the advice of these Pentagon leaders to make informed choices.

Planning is a huge part of what the Pentagon does during wartime. Every mission requires a detailed plan that takes into account the goals, the possible risks, the resources needed, and the challenges that might come up. Planners at the Pentagon think through every possible scenario, figuring out what could go wrong and how to respond if it does. They consider factors like the terrain, weather conditions, and the types of equipment and supplies that will be needed. For example, if troops are going to be in a desert region, planners will make sure there are plenty of water and medical supplies, as well as the right kind of vehicles that can handle the rough terrain and extreme heat. They also plan for backup options, so if the original plan doesn't work as expected, there's a "Plan B" or even a "Plan C" ready to go. This kind of preparation helps keep soldiers as safe as possible and gives them the best chance of completing their mission successfully.

Communication is absolutely essential during wartime, and the Pentagon is responsible for keeping communication lines open, clear, and secure. It's not just about talking; it's about making sure the right information gets to the right people at the right time. Military operations involve many moving parts, and a single misunderstanding could put lives at risk. So, communication experts at the Pentagon make sure that commanders on the ground, naval fleets, and air forces all have access to the latest information. They use highly secure systems to prevent enemies from listening in, and they often rely on technology that's specifically designed for military use. This technology allows the Pentagon to stay in touch with troops even if they are thousands of miles away in challenging environments. Quick and accurate communication is often the difference between success and failure, so it's taken very seriously at the Pentagon.

During wartime, intelligence is key to making informed decisions, and the Pentagon has some of the best intelligence experts in the world working around the clock to provide valuable information. Intelligence analysts gather data from satellites, intercepted communications, and reports from people on the ground, such as spies or allied forces. They look for signs of enemy movement, changes in tactics, or potential threats. For example, if enemy forces are moving closer to an area where

U.S. troops are located, the intelligence team can provide a warning that allows commanders to prepare for an encounter. Intelligence isn't just about knowing what the enemy is doing; it's also about understanding their motivations, resources, and possible strategies. This helps the Pentagon predict what might happen next and adjust its own plans accordingly. The analysts work tirelessly, often under tight deadlines, to give military leaders the information they need to make the best choices for the mission.

Logistics is another area where the Pentagon plays a critical role in wartime. Logistics is all about getting the right supplies, equipment, and people to the right place at the right time. In a war, supplies like food, fuel, medical kits, and ammunition are essential for keeping troops ready and able to complete their mission. The Pentagon's logistics team has to figure out how to transport all these items, even if the location is remote or challenging to reach. They might use planes, ships, trucks, or helicopters, depending on the terrain and urgency. If troops are moving through rough terrain, logistics experts make sure they have the right vehicles and that there's enough fuel available. They even plan for situations where supply routes might be blocked or disrupted, making sure there are alternative ways to get what's needed to the troops. Logistics may seem like a behind-the-scenes job, but it's actually one of the most important aspects of wartime operations because it keeps the whole mission running smoothly.

The Pentagon also has a critical role in providing medical support for troops during wartime. War can lead to injuries, and it's essential to have medical personnel and supplies ready to help wounded soldiers as quickly as possible. The Pentagon coordinates medical teams, including doctors, nurses, and medics, and makes sure they have the resources they need to provide care. They also plan for evacuation routes to quickly move injured troops to safer areas or even back to the United States for more intensive treatment if necessary. In addition to physical health, the Pentagon also provides mental health support for soldiers dealing with the stress and trauma that can come from being in a conflict zone. This kind of care is important because it helps soldiers recover and return to duty if they're able, and it also ensures that they have support for their mental well-being, which is just as important as their physical health.

Technology and innovation play a huge role in the Pentagon's wartime efforts. The Pentagon constantly works on developing new technologies that can give the military an edge, whether it's advanced weaponry, protective gear, or systems that help troops stay connected. For example, drones have become an important tool in modern warfare, allowing the military to gather intelligence or carry out missions without putting people in harm's way. These drones can fly over enemy territory, providing a "bird's-eye view" of what's happening on the ground, which can be extremely valuable for planning and carrying out missions. The Pentagon also invests in cybersecurity to protect sensitive information and communications from enemy hackers. Cybersecurity experts monitor for suspicious activity and use advanced tools to keep military systems secure, which is especially important in a world where digital attacks are becoming more common.

Protecting allies is another critical aspect of the Pentagon's wartime role. The United States often fights alongside other countries, and the Pentagon works closely with these allies to coordinate efforts. When the U.S. and its allies fight together, it's important that everyone's actions are well-coordinated, so the Pentagon helps plan joint missions, share information, and make sure that everyone is working toward the same goals. For instance, NATO is a military alliance that includes the U.S. and many European countries. When NATO forces work together, they train and operate as a unified force, which allows them to respond quickly and effectively to threats. The Pentagon also supports allies by sharing technology, intelligence, and even equipment when needed. This cooperation not only strengthens the mission but also builds trust and partnerships that can last long after the conflict is over.

Once a mission or a conflict is underway, the Pentagon keeps track of everything happening on the battlefield. They receive constant updates from commanders in the field, and they use this information to adjust strategies as needed. If a battle is going differently than expected, the Pentagon can change tactics, send reinforcements, or provide additional resources. This kind of real-time decision-making is essential because war is unpredictable, and conditions can change rapidly. The ability to adapt quickly gives U.S. forces a better chance of achieving their objectives and keeping soldiers as safe as possible. To make these adjustments, the Pentagon has teams of experts who are skilled in analyzing battlefield data and making recommendations based on the latest information.

The Pentagon also has the job of communicating with the public and keeping people informed about what's happening during wartime. They have teams that handle public relations, preparing statements and answering questions from the media. These communication experts provide updates about military operations, explain the reasons behind certain actions, and address any concerns that the public might have. Their work is important because people back home want to know what's happening and why, especially if there are family members or friends involved in the conflict. By keeping the public informed, the Pentagon helps build trust and understanding, which can be especially important during challenging times.

Another important responsibility of the Pentagon during wartime is honoring and supporting the families of soldiers. Many families experience worry and stress when a loved one is deployed to a conflict zone, and the Pentagon works to provide them with resources, information, and support. This includes everything from family readiness programs to financial support and counseling services. The Pentagon understands that military families make many sacrifices, so they strive to offer assistance that can make things a little easier during difficult times. They provide regular updates on soldiers' welfare and, when possible, arrange communication so families can stay in touch. By supporting military families, the Pentagon helps create a strong foundation that allows soldiers to focus on their mission, knowing that their loved ones are being cared for back home.

After a conflict ends, the Pentagon's role doesn't stop. They oversee the process of bringing troops home and helping them transition back to civilian life. This includes providing medical care for any injuries sustained, offering mental health support, and helping veterans find new jobs if they decide to leave the military. The Pentagon works closely with the Department of Veterans Affairs to ensure that all service members receive the support they need after their service. This process is important because transitioning from a conflict zone to everyday life can be challenging, and the Pentagon wants to make sure that soldiers have everything they need to adjust successfully. They also review the conflict to learn valuable lessons that can help improve future operations.

In addition to helping individual soldiers, the Pentagon also reviews the war as a whole to understand what went well and what could be improved. They analyze strategies, examine equipment performance, and consider feedback from commanders and soldiers. This information helps them refine training programs, improve equipment, and adjust their approach for future missions. By learning from each conflict, the Pentagon can better prepare for any future challenges, making sure that the U.S. military is always ready to protect the country.

Through planning, coordination, support, and constant communication, the Pentagon's role in wartime is vast and complex. It involves every step, from the initial decision to enter a conflict to the final stages of bringing troops home and learning from the experience. The people who work at the Pentagon understand the importance of their role, and they dedicate themselves to making sure that every mission is carried out with the best possible strategy, equipment, and support. The Pentagon's work is all about protecting the country and supporting those who serve, and during wartime, this mission becomes even more vital as they work to keep America safe and strong.

Chapter 11: Technology and the Future of Defense

Technology plays a massive role in shaping the future of defense, and the Pentagon is at the center of this constant race to develop new tools, gadgets, and systems to keep the U.S. military strong and ready for any situation. Imagine having the latest high-tech tools to protect not only soldiers on the battlefield but also citizens back home. That's what the Pentagon's technology experts are working toward every single day. They focus on creating technology that can help soldiers be more aware of their surroundings, make better decisions, and carry out missions more safely and effectively. From advanced computers and robots to special protective gear and fast communication systems, technology in defense is always evolving to address new challenges and possibilities.

One of the most exciting areas of technology that the Pentagon is exploring is artificial intelligence, or AI. AI is the technology that allows computers and machines to "think" in some ways like humans do. In the Pentagon, AI is used to process huge amounts of information in a short amount of time, allowing military leaders to understand a situation faster and make quick, informed decisions. For example, AI can analyze satellite images to spot possible threats or unusual activity, helping the military to know if something is happening that might need attention. AI can even predict possible moves by enemies based on patterns from past events, giving leaders a better idea of what to expect. With AI, the Pentagon can sift through endless streams of information, from weather data to troop locations, much more quickly than humans could, making operations faster and safer.

Drones are another incredible piece of technology that the Pentagon has invested in heavily. Drones are unmanned aerial vehicles, which means they don't have a pilot on board—they're controlled remotely or can even fly on their own with programmed instructions.

Drones are used in all kinds of ways by the military, from watching over enemy territory to delivering supplies to soldiers in hard-to-reach places. Some drones are small, flying close to the ground and acting as "eyes in the sky" for soldiers, while others are larger and can fly much higher, covering vast areas to keep an eye on enemy movements or even carry out specific missions. Because they don't have a person on board, drones can go into dangerous areas where it would be too risky to send human pilots, helping to keep soldiers safe.

Another area of interest is cybersecurity. With so much of today's world relying on digital information and communication, protecting military networks from hackers has become a top priority. Cybersecurity experts at the Pentagon are constantly monitoring systems to make sure they're protected from attacks by hackers who might try to steal information or disrupt operations. In a world where enemies could launch a digital attack from anywhere on the planet, cybersecurity is incredibly important for keeping the military's plans and information safe. These experts use sophisticated tools and software to detect suspicious activity and block it before it can cause any harm. They even create "firewalls," which are like digital walls that keep unwanted intruders out. And it's not just about defense; the Pentagon also has teams that are trained in offensive cyber tactics, meaning they can take action to disrupt enemy systems if needed, making cyber warfare one of the newest and most advanced areas in military strategy.

When it comes to communication, the Pentagon knows that clear and fast connections are essential in military operations. New communication technologies allow soldiers, pilots, and commanders to stay connected even in the most remote and difficult locations. The Pentagon uses satellites to make sure messages can be sent from one place to another quickly and securely. Imagine soldiers in the middle of the desert who need to talk to their base miles away or a pilot flying over the ocean who needs real-time information from the ground.

With advanced communication systems, the Pentagon ensures that everyone can stay connected no matter where they are. These systems are built to be resilient, which means they can keep working even in challenging conditions, like bad weather or in areas where there is a lot of interference.

The Pentagon is also working on "smart" gear for soldiers. This includes things like helmets with built-in displays that can show maps, nearby enemies, or even live video feeds from drones flying overhead. Imagine being able to see everything you need to know about a mission right inside your helmet! Some new military suits and uniforms are even designed with sensors that can monitor a soldier's health, checking their heart rate, hydration, and stress levels. This way, if a soldier is injured, medics can know exactly what's wrong even before they get there. These "smart" suits can even communicate with each other, allowing soldiers in a team to share information about what they see or hear, making teamwork easier and more effective. The Pentagon's focus on this kind of technology means that soldiers are more protected and better prepared, with equipment that adapts to their needs on the battlefield.

One of the most futuristic areas the Pentagon is exploring is robotics. Robots can be used in places that are too dangerous for humans, such as defusing bombs, exploring collapsed buildings, or searching for enemy troops in hazardous environments. Some robots are designed to look like small vehicles, and they can travel over rough terrain, climb stairs, or even swim through water to reach their destination. Others are smaller, like robotic arms, which can handle delicate tasks like dismantling explosives. There are even robots that can move and act like animals, such as "robot dogs," which can run over challenging terrain to carry supplies or gather information. The use of robotics not only saves lives by reducing the need to send people into dangerous situations, but it also allows for more precise, reliable work, especially in tasks that require close attention to detail.

Hypersonic technology is another breakthrough that the Pentagon is focusing on. Hypersonic missiles, for example, can travel at speeds faster than five times the speed of sound, which is incredibly fast! These missiles can reach their targets much more quickly than traditional missiles, making it harder for enemies to defend against them. Hypersonic technology could change the way the military approaches both offense and defense, as it allows for rapid responses and makes it very difficult for enemies to react in time. However, developing hypersonic technology requires overcoming huge technical challenges, such as dealing with the intense heat that these fast speeds create. The Pentagon is working closely with scientists and engineers to solve these problems and bring hypersonic technology into regular use, knowing it could give the U.S. military a major advantage.

Another area where the Pentagon is investing a lot of effort is space technology. The military now has a branch called the Space Force, which focuses on protecting U.S. interests in space. This includes monitoring satellites, which are essential for communication, navigation, and gathering intelligence. Space is becoming an important new frontier for defense because countries are increasingly relying on satellites for military and civilian purposes. The Pentagon is working on ways to protect these valuable satellites from attacks, whether from missiles or from cyber threats. They're even exploring the possibility of having military outposts in space or using space-based systems to monitor what's happening on Earth. The idea of using space as a part of defense may sound like something out of a science fiction movie, but the Pentagon is taking it very seriously as technology continues to advance.

In addition to all these exciting technologies, the Pentagon is focused on developing new types of protective gear and medical technology to keep soldiers safe and healthy. For example, they're working on armor that is lighter but still very strong, allowing soldiers to move more easily while staying protected. New medical technology includes portable devices that can help treat injuries right on the battlefield, making it possible to start medical care immediately without waiting for a full hospital setup. There are even futuristic ideas like regenerative medicine, which might one day allow injured soldiers to recover more quickly or even regrow damaged tissue. This focus on health and protection shows that the Pentagon cares about keeping its soldiers safe, not only from enemy attacks but also from the physical challenges of being in a combat environment.

Energy efficiency is another key area for the Pentagon, as the military uses a lot of fuel and power to run its operations. New energy technology, such as solar power and portable energy generators, helps the military operate in remote areas without relying as much on traditional fuel sources. Imagine a group of soldiers in a desert outpost who can use solar panels to power their equipment instead of needing a constant supply of fuel. Not only does this make operations more flexible, but it's also better for the environment. The Pentagon is researching ways to create long-lasting batteries and energy storage systems that can power everything from vehicles to communication equipment. This focus on energy innovation helps reduce costs and makes military operations more sustainable.

One of the most important things about all of this technology is that it has to work together smoothly. That's why the Pentagon invests in systems that allow different technologies to communicate and function as a united network. For example, if a drone is gathering information in a combat zone, that information can be instantly shared with ground troops, command centers, and even other drones or aircraft. This interconnected network allows the military to respond to threats faster and with greater coordination, as each part of the military can instantly know what the others are doing. This system of connected technologies, often called "integrated warfare," makes the U.S. military more effective and more powerful, especially when faced with complex or fast-moving situations.

Looking to the future, the Pentagon knows that staying ahead in technology means constantly learning and improving. That's why they work with universities, technology companies, and other experts to explore the latest discoveries and push the boundaries of what's possible. The Pentagon even funds research projects and runs competitions to inspire new ideas and solutions. By working with people outside of the military, they can bring fresh perspectives and cutting-edge knowledge into defense planning. They're also training the next generation of military and technology experts, teaching them how to use these new tools and think creatively about future challenges.

Ultimately, the Pentagon's use of technology is all about making sure the U.S. military can protect the country effectively, even as the world changes and new threats arise. The future of defense may involve things we can't even imagine today—like artificial intelligence that can make its own decisions, robots that can operate completely independently, or systems that can respond to threats faster than ever. By investing in these advancements, the Pentagon is helping to ensure that the U.S. military stays strong, adaptable, and ready for whatever the future might bring. Through technology, the Pentagon is preparing for a world where battles might look very different from those of the past but where the mission of keeping the country safe remains the same.

Chapter 12: Famous Moments at the Pentagon

The Pentagon, as one of the most important buildings in the United States, has been the site of many historic moments that have shaped the country and its defense strategies. These famous moments aren't just part of the Pentagon's history—they're moments that reflect the challenges, triumphs, and resilience of the nation. From wartime decisions to groundbreaking ceremonies, each of these events tells a unique story about the Pentagon and its role in protecting the United States.

One of the most significant moments in the Pentagon's history was its construction during World War II. When construction began in 1941, the U.S. had just entered the war, and the military needed a central location to organize its defense efforts. Before the Pentagon, military offices were scattered across Washington, D.C., making it difficult for leaders to coordinate and plan quickly. The idea of a single, massive building where all branches of the military could work together was groundbreaking at the time. This building was designed to bring together the Army, Navy, and other defense departments under one roof, and it was planned and built with remarkable speed. Within just 16 months, a building with five sides, five floors, and miles of corridors was ready to house thousands of military personnel and civilian workers. This fast construction showed the determination of the United States to respond to global threats and symbolized the nation's readiness to stand strong during wartime.

The Pentagon also witnessed the end of World War II and the transition into the Cold War era. After World War II ended in 1945, the Pentagon's role changed from managing a global conflict to preparing for the tensions that arose between the U.S. and the Soviet Union. This period was marked by the fear of nuclear weapons and the potential for a large-scale conflict. During the Cold War, the Pentagon became a hub for intelligence operations, military planning, and defense strategies focused on preventing nuclear war. One famous moment during this time was the Cuban Missile Crisis in 1962. The world held its breath as the U.S. discovered Soviet missiles in Cuba, just 90 miles from American shores. Military leaders gathered at the Pentagon to decide the best course of action. After days of tense planning and communication, President John F. Kennedy and his advisors, including military experts from the Pentagon, managed to negotiate with the Soviet Union to remove the missiles from Cuba. This successful resolution prevented a possible nuclear war and showcased the Pentagon's critical role in managing crises and keeping the country safe.

In 1963, the Pentagon again became a focal point during the Vietnam War. This war was different from World War II, with complicated challenges that were difficult for military leaders to solve. Many people in the United States were opposed to the war, and in 1967, thousands of protesters gathered at the Pentagon to call for an end to the conflict. This protest became famous as one of the largest anti-war demonstrations in American history, with around 50,000 people marching on the Pentagon. They stood on the steps of the building, symbolizing the divide between the military and the public at that time. The Pentagon protest brought attention to the impact of the war and eventually influenced the government's decision to end U.S. involvement in Vietnam. This moment is remembered not only as a demonstration but also as a turning point in public opinion about the military and government decisions.

One of the darkest days in the Pentagon's history happened on September 11, 2001. On that day, terrorists hijacked commercial airplanes, two of which were flown into the World Trade Center in New York City, while another was directed toward the Pentagon. The plane crashed into the western side of the Pentagon, causing an explosion and damaging a large part of the building. This attack was the first time the Pentagon had been directly struck, and it brought the horrors of terrorism directly to the nation's capital. Hundreds of people inside the Pentagon were injured, and 125 people were killed, along with the passengers on the plane. But even in the midst of this tragedy, the Pentagon's staff showed courage and resilience. After the initial shock, workers rushed to help each other, providing first aid and evacuating the building. Within hours, the Pentagon was organizing its response, planning rescue efforts, and working with other agencies to address the crisis. The attack on the Pentagon on 9/11 changed the way the building operated, leading to new security measures and a renewed commitment to fighting terrorism. It was a moment of loss but also of bravery and unity as people came together to support one another.

Another famous moment for the Pentagon came in 2003, with the start of the Iraq War. After the events of 9/11, the Pentagon became heavily involved in planning military operations to address global threats. The Iraq War marked the beginning of a new era in U.S. military strategy, as the Pentagon worked to create plans for "preemptive" strikes, which meant acting against threats before they could harm the U.S. The decision to go to war with Iraq was controversial, with many people questioning whether it was the right course of action. Despite the debate, the Pentagon focused on its mission to carry out the operations and support troops on the ground. This conflict was the first to heavily rely on advanced technology, such as drones and satellite imagery, allowing the Pentagon to monitor and manage operations from afar. This technology-driven approach changed the nature of warfare and demonstrated the Pentagon's commitment to adapting to modern challenges.

In 2011, the Pentagon became part of another major moment when it played a role in the mission to capture Osama bin Laden, the mastermind behind the 9/11 attacks. After years of searching, U.S. intelligence finally located bin Laden in Pakistan. The Pentagon helped plan a highly secretive mission that involved Navy SEALs, who were trained for this dangerous task. The mission, called Operation Neptune Spear, was carried out with precision, resulting in the death of bin Laden. This event was a major achievement in the fight against terrorism and brought a sense of closure to many people affected by 9/11. The Pentagon's involvement in this mission underscored its ongoing role in protecting the U.S. from global threats and showed how determination and strategy could lead to successful outcomes in difficult situations.

Beyond warfare and military operations, the Pentagon has also been a place of historic firsts. In 2013, the Pentagon lifted a ban on women serving in combat roles, a decision that was celebrated as a victory for equality. This meant that women could officially hold any position in the military, including those that involved direct combat, opening up new opportunities and recognizing the contributions of women to the armed forces. The Pentagon's decision reflected changing attitudes within the military and in society as a whole, and it allowed women to be recognized for their skills and bravery on the same level as men. This moment at the Pentagon represented progress and the importance of fairness within the military ranks.

One more recent and notable moment at the Pentagon came with the creation of the Space Force in 2019. The Space Force is a new branch of the military focused on protecting U.S. interests in outer space. This decision marked the first time in over 70 years that a new branch had been added to the U.S. military, highlighting the importance of space in modern defense. The Pentagon now oversees not only operations on land, at sea, and in the air, but also beyond Earth's atmosphere. With the creation of the Space Force, the Pentagon showed that it is ready to address the challenges of the future, adapting to new kinds of threats and responsibilities.

These famous moments at the Pentagon reflect its vital role in U.S. history, both as a center of military strategy and as a symbol of the nation's strength and resilience. Each of these events shows a different side of the Pentagon's work—from planning wars to addressing the needs of the military, responding to crises, and even helping to shape social change. The people who work at the Pentagon understand that they are part of something bigger than just a building; they are part of an institution that has been at the heart of the nation's defense through peace, conflict, tragedy, and victory. The Pentagon continues to evolve with each passing year, always aiming to protect the country and support those who serve, making it a place where history is made and remembered.

Chapter 13: Solving Mysteries with Military Intelligence

Military intelligence is one of the most fascinating and secretive parts of the military, and it plays a huge role in solving mysteries that could affect the safety of the entire country. When you hear "military intelligence," you might think of spies, secret agents, and gadgets, but there's much more to it. Intelligence is all about collecting, analyzing, and understanding information that can help protect people and stop dangers before they happen. The Pentagon, as the heart of America's defense, is where much of this intelligence work is planned and organized. This work requires skilled people who know how to gather clues, make sense of complex situations, and solve mysteries in order to keep the United States safe.

One important part of military intelligence is gathering information from different sources, a process called "intelligence collection." There are many ways to do this. For example, some intelligence comes from watching what's happening from above. Satellites orbit high above Earth, capturing images that can show movements of troops, equipment, or anything unusual. Imagine if there's a sudden build-up of military vehicles along a border or if a strange-looking structure appears in a remote area—these images give the Pentagon clues about what might be going on and allow them to investigate further. Drones are another tool used for gathering intelligence. They can fly over areas that are too dangerous for people, capturing videos and taking photos that help intelligence officers see what's happening on the ground without putting anyone in harm's way.

Another source of intelligence is intercepted communications, which is information gathered by listening in on conversations. Sometimes, people from other countries talk over the phone, send emails, or use radio signals to share important plans. Skilled intelligence officers, working with advanced technology, can listen to and decode these messages if they think it's necessary to protect national security. These officers are experts in languages, codes, and even secret symbols that some groups use to keep their messages hidden. The information they uncover can be used to piece together parts of a larger puzzle, helping the Pentagon understand the plans and intentions of people who might want to cause harm. However, listening in on others is done with strict rules and is usually only used when there's a serious concern about safety.

Human intelligence, or HUMINT, involves actual people gathering information by talking to others or observing situations firsthand. This type of intelligence gathering is often done by special agents or soldiers who are trained to blend in and gather information without drawing attention. They might talk to local people in a foreign country to learn about what's happening there, or they might secretly observe an area to see if anything unusual is going on. These intelligence agents are trained in things like languages, customs, and the art of gathering information without raising suspicion. They have to be very careful and follow strict rules, as their work can be risky, especially if they're in a place where they might be in danger if discovered. HUMINT can be very valuable because it provides firsthand details that satellite images or intercepted messages might miss.

Once all this information is collected, the next step is analysis. Intelligence analysts, who work at the Pentagon and other defense agencies, are like detectives who take the clues gathered from different sources and try to solve mysteries. They look at everything carefully and try to connect the dots, finding patterns or details that might explain what's happening or what might happen next. For example, they might notice that certain people have been seen meeting at a specific location, or that supplies are being moved to a certain area. By connecting these observations, they can make predictions and advise military leaders on what actions to take. Intelligence analysts have to be very careful, as one small mistake could lead to the wrong conclusion, so they use a lot of caution and cross-check their information to be as accurate as possible.

Another part of military intelligence involves counterintelligence, which is like playing defense in the intelligence world. While intelligence focuses on gathering information about others, counterintelligence is all about protecting the U.S. from being spied on. The Pentagon and other agencies work hard to make sure their own plans and information stay safe. They use advanced security systems to protect computers and files, and they have special teams that look for any signs that someone might be trying to steal information. Counterintelligence officers also keep an eye on people who might be interested in secrets, like foreign spies. They use their skills to find these spies and stop them before they can get their hands on anything important. In many cases, counterintelligence involves tricks like sending out false information to confuse enemies or setting traps to catch spies in the act.

One famous example of military intelligence at work was during World War II with the cracking of the German Enigma code. The German military used a special code to keep their messages secret, making it hard for anyone to understand their plans. But with the help of mathematicians, linguists, and codebreakers, the Allies managed to figure out the code, allowing them to read German messages. This breakthrough helped the military understand what the enemy was planning, allowing the Allies to stop attacks before they happened and save countless lives. The Pentagon uses similar techniques today, though with even more advanced computers and technology, to decode and understand information that might be hidden in complex ways.

Military intelligence also has a critical role in preventing terrorism. After the attacks of September 11, 2001, intelligence work became even more focused on finding and stopping terrorists before they could carry out their plans. Intelligence officers gather clues about possible threats, monitor suspicious activity, and work with other countries to track down people who might be planning attacks. One example is when intelligence led to the discovery of Osama bin Laden's location in Pakistan in 2011. After years of searching, intelligence analysts pieced together clues and discovered where he was hiding. This led to a mission by Navy SEALs, which successfully ended in capturing bin Laden and dealing a major blow to terrorism. Such missions show how intelligence work requires patience, precision, and teamwork.

In modern times, military intelligence also uses artificial intelligence (AI) and machine learning to handle large amounts of data. AI can quickly scan through information, like satellite images or social media posts, to identify anything unusual or suspicious. This technology helps intelligence officers focus on the most important clues without having to search through endless amounts of data by themselves. Machine learning can also "learn" from patterns, getting better at identifying potential threats over time. For instance, if AI detects that certain actions or movements often lead to a certain type of attack, it can alert intelligence officers to pay closer attention to similar situations in the future. AI doesn't replace human intelligence officers, but it helps them work faster and more effectively.

Another interesting part of intelligence work is using psychological operations, or "psyops." Psyops are methods of using information to influence or even confuse opponents. This can be done by spreading messages or news that might cause enemies to make mistakes or give up. In some cases, the military uses psyops to convince people in a conflict zone to surrender without a fight, saving lives on both sides. Psyops might also involve creating rumors or using media to mislead enemies, making it harder for them to know what's really happening. These operations require creativity and a deep understanding of human psychology, as the goal is to influence how people think and act.

Military intelligence also plays a big role in handling cyber threats, as more attacks now come through digital means. Hackers might try to break into the Pentagon's computer systems to steal information or disrupt operations. Cyber intelligence experts are like digital detectives, using software to track down hackers, protect sensitive information, and prevent cyber attacks. They set up firewalls and encryption to make it difficult for hackers to access important data. They also monitor networks for suspicious activity, catching problems before they become serious threats. This area of intelligence is growing fast because as technology advances, so do the ways that enemies try to use it for harm. Keeping cyber threats under control is now one of the biggest challenges for intelligence officers.

In some cases, military intelligence works alongside other agencies to solve complex mysteries. The CIA, FBI, and other organizations all play roles in gathering intelligence, and when a big threat is identified, they work together to tackle it. This teamwork is essential because different agencies have different skills and resources. For instance, the CIA might gather intelligence overseas, while the FBI focuses on threats within the U.S. By sharing information and resources, they can solve mysteries that might be too difficult for one agency alone. During the hunt for bin Laden, the CIA and military intelligence worked closely together to find clues and plan the mission. Their teamwork showed how important it is for different parts of the government to cooperate on critical missions.

One of the biggest challenges in military intelligence is separating real threats from false leads. With so much information coming in every day, intelligence officers have to be able to tell what's important and what isn't. This is called "analysis and validation," and it requires a lot of skill and experience. Sometimes, clues can be misleading or seem more serious than they really are. Intelligence officers have to investigate carefully and check the facts before they take any action. This careful approach is important because acting on false information could lead to mistakes or unnecessary conflict. By validating every piece of information, intelligence officers make sure that their actions are based on reliable evidence.

Military intelligence is also vital for planning future defenses. Intelligence analysts look at possible threats and imagine what kinds of attacks or challenges might happen in the future. By preparing for these possibilities, they help the Pentagon create strategies that keep the country ready for anything. This process, called "strategic intelligence," involves predicting trends and studying how other countries are improving their own military and technology. By understanding these trends, the Pentagon can develop better defenses and avoid being caught off guard by new threats.

In the end, military intelligence is about using information to solve mysteries that could impact the safety of the country. It involves finding hidden clues, understanding complex situations, and working together to make the best decisions. Whether it's analyzing satellite images, decoding secret messages, or tracking down hackers, intelligence officers are always on the lookout for anything that could pose a threat. Their work is challenging and often unseen, but it's one of the most important ways the Pentagon helps to keep the country safe and ready for whatever might come next.

Chapter 14: The Pentagon in Popular Culture

The Pentagon is one of the most famous buildings in the world, and it has made its way into popular culture in countless ways. Movies, books, TV shows, video games, and even music have featured or mentioned the Pentagon because it represents so much more than just a building. It's a symbol of strength, power, strategy, and sometimes mystery. For many people, the Pentagon stands as a place where the most important and secretive decisions about national defense are made. The fact that it is a five-sided building with a unique shape and that it houses such powerful organizations makes it a popular subject for creators who want to explore themes of war, peace, intelligence, and suspense. Over the years, the Pentagon has inspired stories that capture people's imaginations, drawing them into tales of spies, secret missions, high-stakes decisions, and the inner workings of military power.

In movies, the Pentagon often appears as the headquarters for military operations or as a place where tough decisions are made by generals, officials, and even the President. For example, in the movie *Top Gun*, the Pentagon is behind the scenes of the story, supporting elite fighter pilots as they train for high-risk missions. Though most of the action happens in the skies, the Pentagon's involvement gives a sense of real-world military structure and importance to the story. Similarly, in movies like *Independence Day* and *Transformers*, where the world is threatened by aliens, the Pentagon becomes a command center where leaders make crucial plans to protect the planet. These movies use the Pentagon as a backdrop to show that the situation is serious and that the country's top military minds are involved. The Pentagon adds drama and realism to these stories, making the audience feel like the stakes are incredibly high.

The Pentagon's portrayal in spy and thriller movies is even more fascinating. Films like *Mission Impossible* and the *Jason Bourne* series feature scenes involving intelligence agencies, hidden secrets, and top-secret missions, often hinting at the Pentagon's role in guiding these complex operations. The building is often shown as a place filled with highly classified information, guarded by tight security, with rooms where agents and analysts work on preventing crises and uncovering threats. These movies sometimes even show the Pentagon as a place of conflict, where different government agencies might disagree on how to handle a crisis. This adds drama to the storyline and makes it feel like the people in the Pentagon are not just making decisions but also dealing with their own inner conflicts. Through these portrayals, the Pentagon is seen as a mix of power and mystery, with secrets that audiences find intriguing.

In books, the Pentagon has served as the setting for countless military and political thrillers. Authors like Tom Clancy have written entire series where the Pentagon is at the heart of the action. Clancy's books, such as *The Hunt for Red October* and *Clear and Present Danger*, often feature high-level military officials working from the Pentagon, facing intense challenges as they make decisions that could affect the whole world. These stories give readers a look at the military's perspective on global events, showing how officers and intelligence experts work together to protect the country. These books add detail to the Pentagon's image by describing the corridors, conference rooms, and even the procedures that might take place there, making readers feel like they're getting a behind-the-scenes look at real military operations. This kind of storytelling helps people imagine what it might be like to work in the Pentagon, giving them an idea of the fast-paced, high-pressure environment where decisions are made in the face of danger.

TV shows also love to feature the Pentagon, especially in political dramas. In shows like *The West Wing* and *Madam Secretary*, the

Pentagon is often shown as a place where top officials gather to discuss matters of national security. In these scenes, characters are often seen debating strategies, weighing options, and trying to find solutions to complex problems. The Pentagon represents the government's efforts to protect the country, and these shows use it to give viewers a sense of the constant planning and careful consideration that goes into national defense. By bringing viewers into fictionalized versions of the Pentagon's halls and meeting rooms, these shows make people think about the real-life decisions that happen there. They reveal that the Pentagon isn't just about power; it's about facing difficult choices and the weight of responsibility.

In the realm of science fiction, the Pentagon has taken on some imaginative roles as well. In shows and movies that explore futuristic ideas, the Pentagon is sometimes depicted as a place where new, high-tech weapons are developed or where the military prepares to deal with threats from outer space. For instance, in the movie *WarGames*, a young hacker accidentally gains access to a Pentagon computer system, which nearly leads to a nuclear disaster. This storyline gives the Pentagon a high-tech and almost science-fiction-like role, as a place where computers, intelligence, and technology can create unforeseen problems. In these kinds of stories, the Pentagon represents not just the military's might but also the potential dangers of technology and the need to use it responsibly.

The Pentagon has even appeared in video games, where players can take on the role of soldiers or intelligence officers working to complete missions that protect the country. In games like *Call of Duty*, players may find themselves inside a virtual Pentagon, taking on missions or receiving orders from higher-ups. These games allow players to experience a taste of what it might be like to be involved in military operations and see the Pentagon as a place where important commands are issued. Video games can make the Pentagon seem larger-than-life, with high-stakes missions and exciting storylines that give players a sense of adventure. Through these games, people can experience the thrill of defending their country, even if it's just a simulation. It's a way for players to feel like they're part of something big, and the Pentagon serves as a powerful symbol of authority and action.

The Pentagon's influence goes beyond movies, books, TV, and video games; it's even found its way into music and art. Musicians sometimes reference the Pentagon in their songs, using it as a symbol of power or as a reminder of the military's role in society. For instance, in the 1960s and 70s, during the Vietnam War, some musicians wrote songs that mentioned the Pentagon as a way of protesting the war. These songs reflected the feelings of many people at the time who were questioning the government's decisions and the role of the military. By mentioning the Pentagon, musicians could capture the complex emotions that people felt—feelings of patriotism mixed with the desire for peace. In this way, the Pentagon became more than just a building; it became a part of cultural discussions about war, peace, and the government's responsibilities.

Artists have also used the Pentagon as inspiration, often to make statements about power or war. Some artists create pieces that include the Pentagon as a symbol of authority, while others might use it to question the use of military power. For instance, in art exhibits or installations, the Pentagon might be represented as a five-sided fortress, showing its strength, or it might be used in a more abstract way to make people think about what it represents. Art can make people reflect on the role of the Pentagon and how it impacts not just the U.S., but the entire world. Through art, the Pentagon is seen as a part of the larger conversation about what it means to protect, to fight, and to strive for peace.

Even in everyday language, the Pentagon has become a symbol. When people talk about military decisions or national security, they might say, "The Pentagon has decided," or "The Pentagon is planning." This shorthand shows how deeply the Pentagon is ingrained in

American culture. People understand that "the Pentagon" represents not just a place, but the people and the power within it. When news reporters mention the Pentagon, everyone knows they're talking about the country's military leadership. This shows how much the Pentagon has become part of American consciousness—it's recognized everywhere as the ultimate center of military strength and defense.

In the end, the Pentagon's presence in popular culture reflects the building's significance and the way it captures the imagination. Through movies, books, TV shows, music, art, and even language, the Pentagon has become a powerful symbol of security, strength, and sometimes secrecy. People are fascinated by the idea of a place where so many important decisions are made, where plans are crafted to protect the nation, and where intelligence experts and military leaders work around the clock to ensure the country's safety. Whether it's shown as a command center, a place of mystery, or a symbol of power, the Pentagon's role in popular culture helps people understand the military's importance and gives them a glimpse into the challenges and responsibilities of protecting a nation. Through these stories and portrayals, the Pentagon continues to be more than just a building—it's a part of the stories, dreams, and concerns that shape how people see the world.

Chapter 15: Life Inside the Pentagon Walls

Life inside the Pentagon is a fascinating mix of routine and responsibility, with thousands of people working together to support and protect the country. Imagine a small city that operates around the clock, with halls buzzing with activity, offices filled with people from all branches of the military, and rooms where top officials discuss strategies and solve problems that can impact the world. The Pentagon isn't just a building; it's a place where serious work is done every day by dedicated individuals who have jobs ranging from planning missions to solving complex problems. People who work there take pride in being part of something bigger, knowing that the work they do directly contributes to national security and helps keep millions of people safe.

The Pentagon is massive. With five sides, five floors above ground, and a layout so large it includes over 17 miles of hallways, the building can be tricky to navigate. When people first start working at the Pentagon, they often have to use maps or even ask for directions to find their way around. Each section of the building has its own purpose, from offices and conference rooms to areas dedicated to security and research. Some people say that you could walk from one side of the Pentagon to the other in about seven minutes, but it might take longer if you get lost in the maze-like hallways. People who have been working there for a long time know all the shortcuts and can even find their way in the dark, but newcomers are often amazed at just how big and complex the building is.

Within the Pentagon's walls, there are offices for every branch of the U.S. military: the Army, Navy, Air Force, Marines, and now even the Space Force. Each branch has its own designated areas, with offices where their top leaders and teams work together to organize and plan everything from daily tasks to long-term strategies. The different branches may have unique missions and responsibilities, but they all work together under the same roof, sharing information and coordinating efforts to protect the country. This close collaboration allows them to make quick decisions when needed, ensuring that each part of the military is prepared and ready to act. Sometimes, people from different branches team up to solve complex problems, combining their skills and knowledge to come up with the best solutions. Working so closely together creates a sense of teamwork and unity, as they are all working toward the same goal: keeping the United States safe.

A regular day inside the Pentagon might seem a lot like any other office job in some ways, with people attending meetings, sending emails, and working on computers. But the stakes are much higher, and every task has a purpose related to national defense. People in the Pentagon are constantly analyzing information, studying reports, and preparing for situations that could impact the country. Intelligence analysts review data to understand potential threats, while planners create strategies to respond to those threats. Some teams focus on organizing supplies and equipment, while others work on training and preparing soldiers for their missions. Everything is planned down to the smallest detail because every person's work at the Pentagon can have serious consequences. Each person knows that their job is important, whether they are gathering intelligence, planning missions, or simply making sure that the building itself is secure and functioning properly.

There are also rooms in the Pentagon that are filled with the latest technology, including secure communication systems and advanced computers that help with analyzing data and planning missions. The Pentagon's technology team ensures that these systems are working correctly and keeps everything secure, as one of their biggest concerns is protecting the information they use and share. This is especially important because the Pentagon deals with highly sensitive information that could be harmful if it falls into the wrong hands. For this reason, security inside the Pentagon is extremely strict. Visitors go through layers of security checks, and even employees must follow specific rules to keep information safe. Some areas of the Pentagon are off-limits to most people, with only those who have special clearances allowed to enter. These secure rooms are where the most secret discussions and planning take place, and the people who work there have to be extra careful about keeping information private.

The Pentagon has a unique culture, where discipline and respect are highly valued. Many of the people who work there are current or former military personnel, so they are used to following orders, working in teams, and handling high-stress situations. For them, working in the Pentagon means being part of a team that's bigger than themselves, and they take pride in being able to serve their country in such an important place. Even for those who aren't in the military, the importance of the work being done in the Pentagon is clear. Civilian employees and contractors also play critical roles, from handling finances to managing contracts and ensuring that every part of the Pentagon runs smoothly. Each person's role is respected, and everyone understands that they are part of a larger mission.

One of the most interesting things about the Pentagon is that it functions like a small city, with amenities to help employees with everyday needs so they can stay focused on their work. There are cafeterias, coffee shops, a gym, a post office, a dry cleaner, and even a medical clinic. People who work in the Pentagon can do a lot without ever leaving the building. The Pentagon's food court is popular among employees, with many different options for meals, snacks, and drinks. The food court is often a place where people from different departments can meet casually, discuss their work, and build friendships. In such a large and serious building, these spots for socializing are essential because they give people a chance to relax and recharge. Since many employees spend long hours working there, having these conveniences within the building allows them to stay energized and focused on their duties.

Despite the serious nature of the Pentagon's work, the people inside find moments to connect and even share a laugh. Teams celebrate birthdays, holidays, and special achievements, and some departments have their own traditions. These moments of celebration bring a sense of normalcy to a workplace where so much is at stake. Working at the Pentagon requires a lot of commitment, and for many, the building becomes like a second home. The people who work there form strong bonds, knowing that they are in it together, working to protect the nation. There's a deep sense of camaraderie and support among employees, which is important because their work can be challenging and sometimes even emotionally draining.

The Pentagon also has a tradition of honoring those who have served, and many areas of the building feature memorials and displays that reflect the history and sacrifices made by the military. The Pentagon Memorial, which is outside the building, honors those who lost their lives in the September 11, 2001 attacks, when the Pentagon was struck by a hijacked plane. This memorial is a reminder to everyone who works there of the sacrifices made in service to the country. Inside, there are also halls dedicated to honoring past leaders, soldiers, and heroes, filled with photographs, medals, and artifacts that tell the story of the U.S. military. These displays serve as a source of inspiration and motivation, reminding employees of the legacy they are part of and the importance of their work.

People working in the Pentagon don't always stay in one position or department for long. Many employees, especially those in the military, move to new roles every few years, taking on different responsibilities and challenges. This keeps the work dynamic and helps employees gain a broad understanding of military operations. It's common for people to work in different departments, learning new skills and building a strong network of contacts. This movement helps the Pentagon stay adaptable and ensures that people with diverse skills and perspectives are part of every decision. Those who work in the Pentagon learn to handle change well, and they develop a wide range of skills that make them valuable assets wherever they go.

One of the things that make working in the Pentagon different from other jobs is the sense of history that surrounds it. Every day, employees walk through halls that have witnessed important moments in American history. They may work in rooms where famous generals and presidents have made critical decisions, and they are part of an institution that has shaped the nation's past and will shape its future. This sense of tradition and history is part of what makes life inside the Pentagon special. Employees feel connected to those who came before them, knowing they are carrying on a legacy of service and dedication.

Working at the Pentagon can be demanding, and employees sometimes face stress because of the high expectations and serious nature of their responsibilities. However, there are support systems in place to help them manage these pressures. The Pentagon offers resources like counseling services, support groups, and programs that encourage a healthy work-life balance. Even though the work is important, Pentagon leaders understand that employees need to take care of their well-being to perform at their best. These programs help people handle the unique challenges of working in a place where national security decisions are made daily.

For the people who work there, the Pentagon is more than just a workplace. It's a place of duty, honor, and teamwork, where people from all walks of life come together to protect and serve the country. It's a place filled with history, a symbol of strength, and a constant reminder of the importance of their work. Life inside the Pentagon is challenging, inspiring, and always focused on the mission to keep America safe. Whether they are analyzing intelligence, organizing military resources, or simply helping the building run smoothly, each person in the Pentagon contributes to a powerful, united effort. It's a unique world within five walls, one where the values of dedication, respect, and service are at the core of everything they do.

Chapter 16: How the Pentagon Supports the Armed Forces

The Pentagon is at the heart of the U.S. military's operations, working every day to support the men and women who serve in the Army, Navy, Air Force, Marine Corps, and Space Force. It's not just a building where high-ranking officials meet and make plans; it's the nerve center where thousands of people work behind the scenes to make sure every branch of the armed forces has what it needs to be ready, strong, and capable of defending the nation. Everything from developing new technology and weapons to managing supplies, logistics, and training programs happens through the careful planning and coordination at the Pentagon. Supporting the armed forces is a massive task that requires teamwork, quick problem-solving, and attention to detail, and the people at the Pentagon work around the clock to make it all possible.

One of the Pentagon's primary roles is to make sure that every branch of the military has the right equipment and resources. This means coordinating with manufacturers and suppliers to get the latest gear, weapons, vehicles, and supplies needed for different missions. The Army, for example, needs everything from tanks and helicopters to uniforms and first aid kits. The Navy relies on advanced ships, submarines, and aircraft, while the Air Force needs high-tech fighter jets, bombers, and drones. The Marines require gear that can handle both land and sea missions, and the Space Force is focused on cutting-edge technology to protect America's interests in space. Each branch has unique needs, and the Pentagon ensures that each one has the specialized tools and equipment it requires to be ready for action. This constant flow of equipment and supplies is essential, as military operations depend on being fully stocked and prepared, whether at home or abroad.

Another major responsibility of the Pentagon is to provide the armed forces with training and development opportunities. The Pentagon oversees training programs to ensure that all service members have the skills they need to succeed in their missions. This includes everything from basic training for new recruits to advanced courses for specialized roles, like piloting fighter jets, working with cybersecurity, or leading a squadron. Training doesn't just happen once, either; it's an ongoing process, as soldiers, sailors, pilots, and marines constantly learn new skills to keep up with changing technology and strategies. The Pentagon also organizes joint training exercises, where different branches practice working together on complex missions. These exercises prepare the military to act as a unified team in real situations, helping them respond quickly and efficiently to any challenge. Through rigorous training and preparation, the Pentagon ensures that all members of the armed forces are ready to face difficult situations with confidence and skill.

Supporting the armed forces isn't only about equipment and training; it's also about making sure service members are taken care of. The Pentagon is deeply involved in programs that focus on the well-being of soldiers, sailors, airmen, marines, and guardians, which is the term for members of the Space Force. This includes everything from healthcare to family support services. The Pentagon manages a large system of military hospitals and medical clinics where service members and their families can receive medical care. The Pentagon also provides mental health support, recognizing that military service can be challenging and stressful. Military members have access to counseling services and support groups to help them deal with any difficulties they may face, whether from training, deployments, or other stressful aspects of their jobs. Family support services are also crucial, as many military families face long periods of separation when their loved ones are deployed. The Pentagon offers programs that help families stay connected, manage their finances, and find support during difficult times. By focusing on the health and happiness of service members and their families, the Pentagon strengthens the overall resilience and readiness of the military.

In addition to providing direct support, the Pentagon plays a key role in developing and researching new technology for the armed forces. Military technology is constantly evolving, and the Pentagon is at the forefront of innovation, working with scientists, engineers, and defense contractors to create advanced tools and weapons. From designing faster and more powerful jets to creating robots that can perform dangerous tasks, the Pentagon is always looking for ways to improve the effectiveness and safety of the armed forces. One area of focus is cybersecurity, as protecting information and communication systems is essential to national security. The Pentagon has dedicated teams working to safeguard military networks and develop strategies to defend against cyber threats. Another area of innovation is artificial intelligence, which can help the military analyze data more quickly and make more accurate decisions. By investing in research and development, the Pentagon ensures that the armed forces stay one step ahead, using the latest technology to enhance their capabilities and protect the country.

Logistics and planning are another critical aspect of how the Pentagon supports the military. Every mission, whether it's a training exercise or a real operation, requires detailed planning and coordination. The Pentagon has teams that specialize in logistics, which is the process of organizing and managing resources. For example, if the military needs to send supplies to a remote base overseas, the logistics team at the Pentagon figures out how to get everything there on time and in the right quantities. They arrange transportation, manage fuel supplies, and even plan for unexpected challenges, like bad weather or equipment breakdowns. Logistics experts also ensure that the military has the supplies it needs for ongoing missions, from food and water to ammunition and medical supplies. This behind-the-scenes work is vital for the armed forces, as it allows them to focus on their missions without worrying about running out of resources. Thanks to the Pentagon's careful planning, the military can operate smoothly and efficiently, ready to respond at a moment's notice.

The Pentagon also coordinates with other countries to support the armed forces in global missions. The U.S. military often works alongside allies, such as NATO members, to achieve common goals and promote peace and stability around the world. The Pentagon organizes joint training exercises with other nations, allowing the armed forces to practice working together with soldiers from different countries. These partnerships strengthen relationships and ensure that allies can coordinate effectively in real situations. The Pentagon's diplomats and military leaders meet with representatives from other countries to discuss strategies, share information, and make sure everyone is on the same page. By building strong international relationships, the Pentagon helps create a safer world and ensures that the U.S. military has allies it can rely on in times of need. Working with allies also allows the U.S. to share resources and expertise, making global missions more effective and efficient.

When it comes to defending the homeland, the Pentagon plays a direct role in protecting the country from threats. In times of crisis, such as natural disasters, the military may be called upon to provide assistance, and the Pentagon coordinates these efforts. For example, if there is a hurricane, earthquake, or wildfire, the Pentagon can mobilize military resources to help with evacuation, rescue, and relief efforts. The armed forces have the equipment and skills to reach people in difficult-to-access areas, and the Pentagon helps make sure that troops and supplies are sent where they're most needed. By supporting these disaster response efforts, the Pentagon ensures that the military is ready to protect and assist Americans in emergencies, bringing critical aid to those affected.

One of the Pentagon's most important roles is intelligence gathering, which supports the military by providing information about potential threats. Intelligence officers at the Pentagon analyze data, monitor events around the world, and work with other agencies to predict and prevent problems. This might include gathering information on potential terrorist threats, tracking movements of hostile forces, or observing political changes in other countries. Intelligence helps the military make informed decisions, allowing them to prepare for challenges before they arise. By staying ahead of potential threats, the Pentagon helps protect not only the military but also the entire country. The work of intelligence analysts is crucial for mission success, as it provides the armed forces with the information they need to respond quickly and accurately to any threat.

The Pentagon also supports the armed forces by managing budgets and making sure that resources are used wisely. Running the military is expensive, and the Pentagon oversees a large budget that covers everything from personnel salaries and benefits to the cost of new equipment and training programs. Pentagon officials work to make sure that taxpayer money is spent efficiently, balancing the needs of the military with financial responsibility. This involves setting priorities, reviewing costs, and finding ways to reduce waste. By carefully managing the budget, the Pentagon ensures that the armed forces have the funds they need to operate effectively while respecting the resources of the American people.

Another way the Pentagon supports the military is by setting policies and creating strategies that guide the armed forces' actions. The Pentagon's leaders, including the Secretary of Defense and the Joint Chiefs of Staff, develop policies that outline the goals and responsibilities of the military. These policies provide direction for everything from daily operations to long-term planning. For example, the Pentagon might create a policy focused on cybersecurity to ensure that military computers and networks are protected, or it might establish guidelines for humanitarian missions to help other countries in need. By setting clear policies, the Pentagon helps the armed forces understand their goals and responsibilities, creating a united vision for how they can best serve and protect the nation.

Finally, the Pentagon is responsible for honoring and recognizing the bravery and dedication of military members. This includes awarding medals, providing benefits for veterans, and creating programs that help soldiers transition to civilian life when they leave the military. The Pentagon's commitment to caring for those who serve doesn't end when their military careers are over; they continue to provide support and resources to veterans, helping them find new jobs, receive medical care, and stay connected to the military community. By recognizing the sacrifices and achievements of service members, the Pentagon reinforces the importance of military service and shows appreciation for the hard work and dedication of those who have served.

In all these ways, the Pentagon plays a vital role in supporting the armed forces, ensuring that they have the resources, training, technology, and support they need to protect the United States. It's a place where countless people work together with one goal: to support the brave men and women who defend the country every day. The Pentagon's support allows the military to operate with strength, confidence, and readiness, making it a powerful force capable of responding to any challenge. From the people who plan missions to those who develop new technology and provide care for service members, everyone at the Pentagon contributes to a team that is dedicated to safeguarding the nation and supporting those who put their lives on the line for freedom and security.

Chapter 17: The Green Side of the Pentagon

The Pentagon might be best known as a place of strategy and defense, but it's also making a name for itself in a completely different way: by becoming more environmentally friendly. Although it's one of the largest and most famous office buildings in the world, the Pentagon has a surprising focus on going green, which means finding ways to reduce its impact on the environment. This "green side" of the Pentagon is all about using resources wisely, reducing waste, and looking for new ways to conserve energy. The people working there have recognized that protecting the environment is just as important as protecting the country because a healthy planet contributes to the health and well-being of everyone, including future generations.

One of the Pentagon's biggest efforts toward being green is in conserving energy. The building is huge, with over 6 million square feet of office space, so powering, heating, and cooling it takes a lot of energy. Over the years, the Pentagon has taken steps to use energy more efficiently, which means finding ways to get the same amount of work done using less power. This is not only good for the environment, but it also saves money. For example, the Pentagon has installed energy-efficient lighting in many of its rooms and hallways. These lights use less electricity than traditional bulbs and last longer, so they don't have to be replaced as often. In addition to better lighting, the Pentagon has also upgraded its heating and cooling systems, which use advanced technology to keep temperatures comfortable while using as little energy as possible. By making these changes, the Pentagon has been able to significantly reduce the amount of energy it uses every day.

Another way the Pentagon is going green is by using renewable energy sources. Renewable energy is energy that comes from natural sources that can be replaced, like sunlight, wind, and water. The

Pentagon has made efforts to include solar power in its energy plan. Solar panels have been installed on some of the buildings around the Pentagon, and these panels capture sunlight and turn it into electricity that can be used to power lights, computers, and other equipment. By using solar energy, the Pentagon is reducing its reliance on fossil fuels, which are non-renewable sources of energy that can harm the environment by releasing pollution. Using renewable energy not only helps reduce pollution, but it also makes the Pentagon more resilient, as it can generate some of its own power instead of relying entirely on energy from outside sources.

The Pentagon also takes water conservation seriously. Water is a precious resource, and conserving it means using it carefully so there's enough for everyone, including future generations. At the Pentagon, water-saving measures have been put into place to reduce the amount of water used for things like landscaping, cleaning, and cooling systems. For instance, the Pentagon has implemented a system to collect and reuse rainwater, a method called rainwater harvesting. This rainwater can be used for things like watering plants or even cooling some of the building systems, which means less need to use fresh water from local sources. Additionally, the Pentagon has updated its plumbing fixtures, like sinks and toilets, with water-saving models that use less water per flush or per use. These simple changes make a big difference when added up across such a large building.

Speaking of plants, the Pentagon has also made its landscaping greener. The Pentagon sits on a large piece of land, and maintaining the grounds requires a lot of work. Instead of planting grass and plants that need a lot of water, fertilizers, and pesticides, the Pentagon's landscaping team has started using native plants that are better suited to the local environment. Native plants are plants that grow naturally in a particular area, so they're already adapted to the local climate and soil. This means they need less water, less maintenance, and fewer chemicals to keep them healthy. By choosing these types of plants, the

Pentagon reduces its need for water and harmful chemicals, creating a more eco-friendly landscape. Not only does this help conserve resources, but it also supports local wildlife, like bees and butterflies, which rely on native plants for food and habitat.

Reducing waste is another important part of the Pentagon's green initiatives. Every day, thousands of people work at the Pentagon, which means there's a lot of waste generated, from paper and plastic to leftover food and packaging. To tackle this, the Pentagon has set up a strong recycling program that encourages everyone in the building to separate recyclable materials from regular trash. Recycling bins are located throughout the building, making it easy for employees to recycle paper, plastic bottles, aluminum cans, and other materials. By recycling, the Pentagon can reduce the amount of waste that ends up in landfills, which are places where trash is buried and can take many years to break down. Recycling also saves resources, as materials like paper and plastic can be turned into new products instead of requiring new resources to make more.

The Pentagon has also worked to cut down on the amount of paper used within the building. Paper might seem like a small thing, but when thousands of people are using it every day, the amount adds up quickly. By promoting a "paperless" workplace, the Pentagon encourages people to use digital documents instead of printing everything on paper. Many departments now use electronic files, emails, and online forms to share information, which not only saves paper but also makes it easier to organize and access important information. When paper must be used, the Pentagon encourages people to print on both sides of the page and to use recycled paper products whenever possible. Reducing paper waste helps save trees and reduces the amount of energy and water needed to produce new paper, making it an important step in protecting the environment.

Another interesting part of the Pentagon's green initiatives is its focus on sustainable transportation. Because the Pentagon is a huge workplace with thousands of employees, a lot of people travel to and from the building every day. The Pentagon encourages employees to use public transportation, carpool, or even bike to work if possible. There are dedicated parking spaces for carpoolers, bike racks, and even a metro station nearby to make it easier for people to use eco-friendly options. By reducing the number of cars on the road, the Pentagon helps decrease air pollution and the amount of fuel used. Some employees also use electric vehicles, which don't release pollution, and the Pentagon has installed charging stations for these vehicles, making it easier for people to choose cleaner transportation options.

The Pentagon is also focused on creating a healthy indoor environment for everyone who works there. Indoor air quality is important because people spend a lot of time indoors, and breathing clean air helps them stay healthy. The Pentagon has installed air filtration systems that help reduce pollutants and allergens in the air. These systems remove particles like dust, pollen, and other tiny pollutants, making the air cleaner and fresher. Additionally, the Pentagon uses eco-friendly cleaning products that are less harmful to the environment and safer for people to be around. These products don't contain harsh chemicals that can cause health issues, and they help keep the building clean without releasing harmful fumes into the air. This focus on a healthy indoor environment not only supports the well-being of employees but also reduces the Pentagon's overall environmental footprint.

The Pentagon has even looked at the food served in its cafeterias as part of its green efforts. Offering food options that are environmentally friendly helps reduce waste and supports sustainable food practices. Some cafeterias at the Pentagon offer locally sourced food, which means the food is grown or produced close to the building. Locally sourced food doesn't have to travel as far, which reduces transportation costs and pollution. Additionally, the Pentagon encourages people to use reusable utensils, plates, and cups instead of disposable ones that create waste. Some cafeterias even compost food scraps, which means they turn leftover food into nutrient-rich soil rather than sending it to a landfill. Composting is a natural way to recycle food waste, and it helps improve soil for future plant growth.

Sustainability is a big part of the Pentagon's renovations and updates. Whenever a new area of the building is renovated, the Pentagon tries to use sustainable building materials, such as recycled or environmentally friendly products. This means that when old materials are replaced, they are often recycled, and new materials are chosen based on how eco-friendly they are. For example, during some renovations, materials like recycled steel, sustainable wood, and low-VOC (volatile organic compound) paints are used. Low-VOC paints release fewer harmful chemicals into the air, making them better for both people and the environment. By making these choices, the Pentagon is ensuring that its future renovations have a smaller impact on the planet.

One of the most important parts of the Pentagon's green efforts is educating employees about environmental responsibility. The Pentagon organizes programs and events that teach people about how they can make a difference by conserving energy, reducing waste, and being mindful of the resources they use. These programs encourage employees to think about their daily actions and how small changes, like turning off lights when leaving a room or recycling a plastic bottle, can add up to make a big difference. The Pentagon also celebrates events like Earth Day, where employees participate in activities focused on protecting the planet. By involving everyone in these efforts, the Pentagon creates a culture of sustainability, showing that every person can help make the environment healthier.

The Pentagon's green initiatives are a reminder that even the biggest buildings with serious responsibilities can take steps to protect the planet. By focusing on energy efficiency, water conservation, waste reduction, sustainable transportation, and environmental education, the Pentagon is making an effort to create a workplace that respects both people and the planet. This commitment to sustainability shows that the Pentagon cares about the future, not only of national security but also of the environment. It's a way for the building to set an example for others, proving that any place—no matter how large or complex—can take steps to become greener and more environmentally responsible.

In many ways, the Pentagon's efforts to go green are just as important as its other responsibilities. By protecting the planet, the Pentagon is helping to protect the health and well-being of the American people. As new technologies and ideas emerge, the Pentagon will continue to look for ways to make its operations even more sustainable, ensuring that this legendary building is a leader in both defense and environmental stewardship.

Chapter 18: The History of the Pentagon's Construction

The story of how the Pentagon was built is like a tale of determination, creativity, and urgency, all mixed into one. The Pentagon's construction began during a very tense time in history—the start of World War II. In the early 1940s, the United States realized it needed a new kind of headquarters to house the growing number of military personnel and activities as the nation prepared for war. Before the Pentagon was built, the Department of War (now the Department of Defense) was scattered in different buildings across Washington, D.C. This spread-out setup made it difficult for officials to communicate quickly and work together efficiently. As the threat of war loomed closer, military leaders needed a solution—and fast.

President Franklin D. Roosevelt understood that a new building was essential, one that would bring all the key military offices together in a single location. In 1941, he approved a plan for a headquarters that could hold all the people and resources necessary for coordinating the defense of the United States. There was just one problem: the new building had to be built quickly and on a budget, which was no easy task for a project of such an enormous scale. Military planners got to work immediately, designing a building that could house about 40,000 workers and that would be large enough to serve as the central hub for U.S. defense.

One of the first challenges was deciding where to build this massive headquarters. They chose a location in Arlington, Virginia, just across the Potomac River from Washington, D.C. The chosen spot was an area known as Arlington Farm, which had mostly flat, unused land that was ideal for constructing a large building quickly. However, there was a complication: the nearby Arlington Cemetery, a national military cemetery, was just across the road. This meant that the building could not be too tall or block the view of the cemetery. Planners had to think creatively about how to fit such a large structure without disrupting the area around it.

As the team brainstormed designs, they decided on a unique shape that would maximize space without creating a building that was too tall. Thus, the idea of a five-sided building was born. The Pentagon shape allowed the planners to create five rings of office space, connected by corridors that made it easy for workers to move between different parts of the building quickly. This design also meant that the building could be shorter and cover more ground horizontally, rather than towering vertically and blocking views of the cemetery.

With the design finalized, construction began on September 11, 1941. Right from the start, the builders faced an ambitious timeline: the U.S. was racing against time, knowing that it might soon be involved in World War II. The government set a tight deadline of one year to complete the building. For a project of this size, this was nearly unheard of. Typically, constructing such a large building would take several years, but because of the urgency, every aspect of the construction process had to be carefully planned and efficiently managed. The architects, engineers, and construction workers on the project knew they had no time to waste.

To speed up the process, the builders used a technique called "fast-tracking." This meant that different parts of the building were constructed simultaneously instead of one after another. For example, while workers were laying the foundation, other teams were already starting to build the walls in another section. This method allowed construction to happen quickly, but it required a lot of coordination to make sure all the pieces fit together properly. Another strategy was to use reinforced concrete instead of steel, as steel was in short supply due to the war effort. Concrete was cheaper and easier to get, and it also made the building strong and fire-resistant, which was important for a facility meant to withstand potential threats.

As the work continued, thousands of construction workers joined the project, creating a bustling site filled with the sounds of hammers, drills, and machinery. The workers toiled day and night to meet the deadline. Despite the urgency, the builders paid close attention to the quality of the work, ensuring that the structure would be solid and reliable. The builders used over 680,000 tons of sand and gravel from the Potomac River, turning it into concrete for the walls and floors. This decision not only saved time and money, but it also ensured that the building would be resilient and last for many years.

In December 1941, just a few months after construction began, the United States was drawn into World War II after the attack on Pearl Harbor. This event made the construction of the Pentagon even more critical. The war intensified, and military leaders were eager to move into a central location where they could make quick, coordinated decisions. With the pressure mounting, the workers doubled their efforts. By early 1942, parts of the building were already in use, even though the entire structure was not yet finished. Workers and military personnel moved in as soon as sections were completed, marking a rare case where people were working in a building that was still under construction.

On January 15, 1943, the Pentagon was officially completed, just 16 months after the groundbreaking ceremony. It had been a remarkable achievement. The Pentagon, with its five sides, five floors, and five concentric rings of offices, was unlike any other building in the world. Its design allowed it to hold thousands of employees and gave them the ability to walk from one side of the building to the other in just seven minutes—a feat that would have been nearly impossible in a traditionally shaped building of similar size. The total cost of the project was around $83 million, which was a significant amount of money at the time but a fraction of what it would have cost if they had taken the usual several years to complete it.

Since its completion, the Pentagon has remained an architectural marvel and an icon of U.S. military strength. It has housed countless military leaders, strategists, and support personnel, serving as the nerve center for defense planning and operations. Over the years, the Pentagon has been renovated and updated, but the original five-sided design and its core purpose have remained the same. The story of its construction reflects the determination and ingenuity of the people who made it possible, showing how, even under immense pressure and limited resources, a massive, complex structure could be built to meet a country's urgent needs.

Today, when people look at the Pentagon, they see not just a building but a symbol of resilience, unity, and American resolve.

Chapter 19: How the Pentagon Keeps America Safe

The Pentagon is like the brain of America's defense system, coordinating all the actions and decisions needed to keep the country safe. It's home to the Department of Defense, which is in charge of the military branches: the Army, Navy, Air Force, Marines, and Space Force. Each of these branches has a different job, but they all work together to protect the nation from threats both on U.S. soil and abroad. The Pentagon's job is to make sure that these branches have the resources, training, and planning they need to carry out their missions successfully. Inside the Pentagon, thousands of people work every day on tasks that range from developing new defense strategies to maintaining advanced technology and equipment. It's a place where experts in strategy, intelligence, and technology come together to solve problems and stay ahead of any possible threats.

One of the biggest ways the Pentagon keeps America safe is by planning and preparing for a wide range of potential threats. Whether it's a conflict with another country, a terrorist attack, or a natural disaster, the Pentagon is always developing and updating plans to deal with these situations. Experts at the Pentagon study information from around the world, looking at things like international relations, political changes, and technological advancements to figure out what kinds of challenges the country might face in the future. This process is called strategic planning, and it's a bit like playing chess, where each move has to be carefully thought out based on what the opponent might do. By looking ahead, the Pentagon can put plans in place so that the military is ready to respond quickly and effectively if something happens. It's about being proactive instead of waiting until a problem arises.

The Pentagon also supports America's allies, which means other countries that share similar values and work together with the U.S. on defense and security issues. By working closely with allies, the Pentagon helps create strong partnerships that make it easier to respond to global challenges. These partnerships are important because they allow the U.S. to share resources, information, and technology with other countries, making everyone stronger. For example, if there is a situation in a certain part of the world, the U.S. can work with its allies in that region to address it together, rather than trying to handle it alone. These alliances also help deter threats, as potential adversaries know that they would be facing not just one country but a group of united nations. This network of alliances, like NATO (the North Atlantic Treaty Organization), is a key part of the Pentagon's approach to keeping America and its allies safe.

Intelligence gathering is another critical function of the Pentagon. Intelligence is all about collecting information on potential threats or dangerous situations and analyzing it to make smart decisions. The Pentagon has teams of experts who work in intelligence, using a mix of human resources, technology, and international partnerships to gather information. They collect data from satellite images, intercepted communications, and on-the-ground reports, then analyze this information to see if there are any signs of danger. For example, if there are unusual military movements in another country, or if certain individuals are planning an attack, the intelligence teams can detect these patterns and report them. This information helps the Pentagon and other leaders make informed decisions about how to respond or prevent a threat. Intelligence is like the eyes and ears of America's defense system, allowing the Pentagon to stay informed and ready to act.

The Pentagon also plays a major role in protecting the country from cyber threats. In today's digital age, much of our information and infrastructure—like power grids, communication systems, and financial networks—is online. This makes it vulnerable to cyber attacks from hackers or even other countries. The Pentagon has a special branch called the Cyber Command that focuses entirely on cybersecurity. Their job is to defend the country's networks from cyber attacks and, if needed, to launch counter-attacks to disable any systems trying to harm the U.S. Cyber Command experts use cutting-edge technology to detect and stop threats, sometimes even before they happen. They work closely with other agencies, like the FBI and CIA, to ensure that information and resources are shared across different parts of the government. Cybersecurity is a big part of the Pentagon's mission because keeping information safe is just as important as defending physical locations.

In addition to these efforts, the Pentagon is also involved in what's called disaster response and humanitarian assistance. When natural disasters like hurricanes, earthquakes, or floods occur, the Pentagon can provide resources to help affected areas recover. This support often comes from the National Guard and the military, who can be quickly deployed to deliver food, water, medical aid, and other essentials. The Pentagon has the logistics and equipment necessary to reach places that are difficult to access, and their rapid response can make a big difference in saving lives and helping communities get back on their feet. Although disaster response is not a military action, it's a crucial part of keeping Americans safe and is something the Pentagon does to support people in times of need.

Another aspect of the Pentagon's role in national security is training and equipping the military. This involves providing everything that soldiers, sailors, pilots, and other military personnel need to do their jobs effectively. The Pentagon oversees training programs that prepare military members for a wide variety of situations, from combat missions to peacekeeping efforts. They also manage the procurement process, which is how the military gets equipment like tanks, aircraft, ships, and advanced technology. By ensuring that service members are well-trained and well-equipped, the Pentagon gives the military the best possible chance of success in any mission. This training isn't just about physical readiness; it also includes mental preparation, leadership skills, and teamwork, which are essential for handling the stress and challenges of military work.

Research and development (R&D) is another big focus for the Pentagon. R&D is all about creating new technology and finding innovative ways to improve existing equipment and strategies. The Pentagon's R&D efforts have led to the development of advanced technologies like stealth aircraft, unmanned drones, and night-vision goggles, which give the U.S. military a significant advantage. The Pentagon works with scientists, engineers, and private companies to come up with new tools that can help protect the country. These innovations are not just limited to weapons; they also include things like medical technology to treat wounded soldiers and communication systems that allow for secure and fast information sharing. By investing in R&D, the Pentagon ensures that the military stays ahead of potential threats and is always improving.

The Pentagon is also responsible for overseeing the country's nuclear arsenal. Nuclear weapons are the most powerful weapons in the world, and their use would have devastating consequences. Because of this, the Pentagon's job is to maintain these weapons and ensure they are secure, while also working to prevent other countries from using nuclear weapons irresponsibly. This requires a lot of planning, as well as coordination with international organizations to keep track of nuclear materials worldwide. While nuclear weapons are considered a last resort, their presence plays a role in what is known as "deterrence," which means discouraging other countries from attacking the U.S. out of fear of retaliation. The Pentagon's careful handling of the nuclear arsenal is a vital part of keeping the country safe.

Another unique way the Pentagon keeps America safe is through public outreach and education. The Department of Defense, with the

Pentagon at its center, wants Americans to understand the role of the military and to feel connected to those who serve. They organize programs that educate people about national security and sometimes hold public events where people can learn more about the Pentagon and its work. The Pentagon also supports initiatives that help military families, which is important because families play a big role in supporting service members who are deployed or in training. By building this connection with the public, the Pentagon helps foster a strong sense of support and understanding between the military and the American people.

The Pentagon's leadership also plays a huge role in keeping America safe. The Secretary of Defense, who is the head of the Department of Defense, works closely with the President and other government leaders to make major decisions about the country's defense. This leadership team is responsible for developing policies that shape how the military operates, both at home and abroad. They are constantly analyzing information, considering new threats, and planning the best ways to respond. In addition, the Pentagon's leaders work with Congress to secure the funding needed for the military's activities and projects. This ensures that the Pentagon has the resources to carry out its mission effectively. These leaders make important decisions that affect the entire country, and their guidance helps steer the Pentagon's actions toward a future where America remains safe and secure.

Every day, thousands of people at the Pentagon work together to keep America safe, and they are constantly adapting to new challenges and finding ways to improve. With so many different teams focused on a wide variety of tasks, the Pentagon is able to handle everything from protecting against cyber attacks to responding to natural disasters. It's a place where planning, intelligence, technology, and teamwork all come together, creating a powerful defense system that watches over the country. The people who work at the Pentagon know that their job is important, and they take their responsibilities very seriously.

Whether they are planning missions, developing technology, gathering intelligence, or supporting military families, each person at the Pentagon contributes to a mission that is bigger than themselves. They are all part of a team dedicated to keeping America safe now and in the future.

Chapter 20: A Day in the Life of a Pentagon Worker

Imagine starting your day as a worker at the Pentagon, one of the busiest, most secure, and mysterious buildings in the world. Whether you're a soldier, an officer, an analyst, a planner, or an office assistant, your day will be packed with important tasks that help keep the United States safe. Many people who work at the Pentagon have to arrive very early in the morning because the work never stops here. Security is extremely tight, so when you arrive, the first thing you'll do is go through a series of security checks to make sure everything is safe. There are metal detectors, identification checks, and special badges that every worker needs to enter the building. Each person's badge not only identifies who they are but also tells the security team which parts of the Pentagon they're allowed to access, since not everyone is allowed everywhere in the building. These strict security measures keep the Pentagon safe, ensuring that only authorized people can enter.

Once inside, a Pentagon worker might stop by one of the many cafés or dining areas to grab a quick coffee or breakfast before starting their tasks. Since the Pentagon is so big, it has its own food courts with various options to make sure the thousands of people who work there have plenty of choices for meals. After a quick bite, it's time to get started on the day's work, which might look different depending on what the worker's job is. For example, an intelligence analyst might start their day by checking the latest reports from all over the world. They'll read through information collected by satellites, listening devices, and field agents stationed in different countries. By looking for patterns and unusual activities, they help predict potential threats and keep everyone in the building updated on what's happening around the world.

For military officers and planners, a day at the Pentagon could begin with a morning briefing. A briefing is a type of meeting where they discuss important information about national security and defense. These meetings often include top officials from different branches of the military and other government agencies, and sometimes even the Secretary of Defense. During these briefings, Pentagon workers review recent events, examine any new threats or developments, and make decisions about what actions to take. This could include anything from moving troops to a certain location to making plans for humanitarian aid or peacekeeping missions. These meetings are crucial because they allow everyone to stay on the same page and coordinate efforts effectively. A lot of planning and thinking goes into each decision, as these actions can have a big impact on the country and even the world.

Some workers spend their day working on computers and communicating with people across the country and around the globe. These are the workers who handle information, logistics, and technology, making sure everything is running smoothly. For example, some people work on cybersecurity, protecting the Pentagon's computers from potential hackers. Others might work on logistics, which means organizing the transportation of supplies and equipment that the military needs. They figure out how to get food, medical supplies, vehicles, and other resources to the right places at the right times. The Pentagon has a vast network of people who make sure everything is in the right place, and it's a job that requires a lot of organization and problem-solving.

Meanwhile, other workers might be focused on creating strategies and plans. This is especially true for military strategists, who are constantly studying how to respond to different scenarios. They spend their day researching, brainstorming, and developing ideas for what the U.S. should do if a conflict arises. This job requires a deep understanding of world events, politics, and geography, as well as a lot of creativity and critical thinking. These strategists work closely with military leaders, and their plans could involve anything from sending out ships to protect U.S. waters to preparing for cyber threats. Their work involves examining possible outcomes for each decision and predicting how different countries or groups might respond.

For Pentagon workers in the intelligence field, part of the day might be spent meeting with colleagues to discuss new information that has been gathered. Intelligence analysts are like detectives, piecing together clues from different sources. They work with maps, data, photos, and sometimes even intercepted communications. Their goal is to find out what might be happening in other countries that could affect U.S. security. Sometimes, these meetings reveal information that requires immediate attention, like if there's a potential threat that needs to be addressed quickly. These analysts help make sure the Pentagon and military leaders are always informed, allowing them to make decisions based on the best possible information.

If you're a high-ranking military officer at the Pentagon, your day will likely involve a lot of meetings and decision-making. Officers hold discussions with leaders from the Army, Navy, Air Force, and Marine Corps to go over new missions, budget decisions, and personnel needs. They often meet with the Secretary of Defense and even the President to talk about pressing issues. Part of an officer's job is to make sure that all the different branches of the military are working together toward the same goals. For example, if the Air Force is planning a mission, the Army and Navy need to know about it so they can provide any needed support. These high-ranking officials make sure that everything is coordinated across all the branches, and their decisions can have a huge impact on national security.

For civilian employees who work at the Pentagon, a day might be focused on supporting these military operations in other ways. Some civilians work on budgets, managing how much money is spent on equipment, technology, and personnel. Others might be involved in research and development, working on new technologies to improve the military's capabilities. There are even people who work on environmental efforts, making sure the Pentagon operates in a way that's as eco-friendly as possible. Civilian employees are essential to the Pentagon's daily functions, as they bring expertise from various fields like engineering, law, and medicine. They work alongside military personnel, and together they create a team that's well-equipped to handle a wide range of tasks.

When it's time for lunch, Pentagon workers have a few options. They can visit one of the food courts in the building or grab a quick meal at one of the cafés. Since the Pentagon is like a small city, there are plenty of places to eat without ever leaving the building. Some workers might even take a quick walk around the inner courtyard, which is a big open space in the middle of the Pentagon's five sides. The courtyard is a place where people can take a break, get some fresh air, and chat with colleagues before going back to work.

Afternoon activities might involve more meetings, project work, or training sessions. The Pentagon has state-of-the-art classrooms where workers can attend courses to learn about the latest developments in defense technology, leadership skills, or global affairs. Training is a big part of working at the Pentagon, as it's important for everyone to stay up-to-date with new information and techniques. In fact, Pentagon workers are often among the first to learn about new technologies and methods in defense, so they're constantly improving their skills and knowledge.

For some workers, part of the day might be spent working with advanced technology. The Pentagon has labs and tech centers where scientists and engineers test new devices and equipment. Some workers might be testing new protective gear for soldiers, while others are working on robotics, artificial intelligence, or cybersecurity tools. These projects are essential for keeping the U.S. military ahead of other countries in terms of technology. These workers are always innovating and finding ways to improve defense systems, making sure the U.S. has the most advanced tools available.

As the day goes on, some workers might receive briefings or updates on ongoing missions around the world. These briefings are like mini reports that provide the latest information on military operations, troop movements, and international developments. For instance, if there's a situation in another country, Pentagon workers might get updates on what's happening, what actions are being taken, and any new risks that might arise. These briefings help everyone stay informed and make sure that the right people are ready to respond if needed.

Toward the end of the day, Pentagon workers might take some time to review their work, prepare reports, or set goals for the next day. Many of the tasks done at the Pentagon require a lot of attention to detail and organization, so workers often spend time making sure everything is in order. This might mean updating files, sending important emails, or reviewing notes from meetings. Pentagon workers need to keep track of a lot of information, so organizing and preparing is a key part of their job.

After a long day, Pentagon workers start to head home, but the building never truly sleeps. Even though many workers leave in the evening, others come in to take their place, ensuring that the Pentagon is staffed 24/7. There are always people working, watching, and analyzing information to keep America safe. The day-to-day work at the Pentagon may be challenging and intense, but it's also rewarding, as everyone who works there knows they are contributing to something bigger than themselves. Whether it's through strategy, planning, research, or support, each worker plays an essential role in protecting the country, making a day at the Pentagon a blend of responsibility, teamwork, and purpose.

Epilogue

Now that you've explored the Pentagon, you know it's much more than a big, five-sided building. It's a place where ideas, strategies, and teamwork come together to protect and serve. The Pentagon represents courage, planning, and the strength to face challenges, not only for America but also as an example to the world.

The people working inside the Pentagon are just like you—they're curious, determined, and want to make a difference. From scientists to analysts to the brave men and women of the armed forces, everyone plays a part. And although you may not see their work every day, their dedication and commitment help shape a safer world.

As you close this book, think about what you can bring to your community. Whether it's teamwork, creative ideas, or simply being curious about the world, you have the power to make a difference too. Maybe someday you'll create plans, solve problems, or work with others to help protect and improve the world around you.

The Pentagon is a place filled with history and purpose, but the journey of learning and discovery doesn't end here. The next generation—including readers like you—will shape the future. So, keep exploring, stay curious, and remember that each of us has a part to play in making the world a better place. Who knows? One day, you might even walk the halls of the Pentagon yourself!

The End.

Milton Keynes UK
Ingram Content Group UK Ltd.
UKHW030905011224
451693UK00001B/80